Images of
Ashford

Mike Bennett

Breedon Books
Publishing Company
Derby

First published in Great Britain by
The Breedon Books Publishing Company Limited
Breedon House, 44 Friar Gate, Derby, DE1 1DA.
1998

ISBN 1 85983 123 0

Printed and bound by Butler & Tanner Ltd., Selwood Printing Works, Caxton
Road, Frome, Somerset.

Colour separations by Freelance Repro, Leicester.

Jackets printed by Lawrence-Allen, Avon.

Contents

ACKNOWLEDGEMENTS

Most of the illustrations in this book come from the extensive newspaper archives. They have been taken over the years by many staff photographers who have become familiar faces in the local community.

But in addition grateful thanks must be recorded to readers who have readily loaned pictures for publication. In particular help has been offered from the substantial collections of Stephen Salter of Kennington, Norman Newton of Willesborough and George Weaver of Tenterden.

Other pictures and expert advice has come from many individuals and thanks are due to Philip Paine of Sevenoaks, Peter Oliver of Kennington, Bill Brown of Chartham, Margaret Isaac of Willesborough, Hal Foster of Mersham, Mrs M. Puttock of Tunbridge Wells, Clive Raynes of Newington, Ann Addy of Woodchurch, E. H. Crouch of Ashford, Laurie Humphreys of Ashford and Jonathan Bennett of Tenterden.

In researching the text I have referred to a wide variety of newspapers from the Kent Messenger Group files, and a number of books and pamphlets available in the splendid reference section of Ashford Library.

Introduction

THIS book and its illustrations seek to record the rapid changes in the life and times of Ashford over the past six decades of development from quiet country market town to modern industrial and transport hub of East Kent well prepared for the exciting challenges of the 21st century.

It is a story which shows both the growth and destruction of the area as the rapid pace of change quickly developed Ashford to a place of strategic importance both national and international. Views will vary as to whether the progress has been justified, but what is certain is that the growing demands of development will continue to alter the face of the borough as we move into the new Millennium.

The aim is to give a taste of life in the area during these times of major disruption, particularly in the terrible times of war and the years since.

It is not a comprehensive history but intends to show some of the things we have lost and others that have been gained.

We must go back to the last century to record the first major changes. For centuries the town has stood as a centre of farming interest, with market rights granted in 1242 by Henry III for the selling of 'all manner of goods and beasts' in the long wide High Street.

When the town was chosen by the South-Eastern Railway Company for its main line from Folkestone to London, with junctions to Canterbury and Hastings – and later Maidstone – it signalled a major change in fortune.

Here in Ashford it was decided that the railway works would be developed and that was to be the start of the modern industrial revolution of the area. In 1846 James Wall sold 185 acres of farmland for £21,000 to the railway company. Eighteen months later the Railway Engineering Company opened at Newtown with its elegant clock tower entrance, which still stands today.

That development was the first to completely alter the character of the town and it brought a major increase in population from around 3,000 in 1841 to more than 13,000 in 1901 with a large percentage dependent on the railway for survival.

The railway company erected homes, a school and a pub in a new community of Alfred Town that developed into the Newtown area which still exists, although greatly updated, today. It remained the dominant provider and by the turn of the century Ashford was a 'railway town' of great importance, and it continued to be so until the middle of this century.

The story of the war years in front-line Ashford, in those never to be forgotten days during six years of conflict, was one of extraordinary resolve and determination to continue to live a normal life despite the daily danger.

At the start of the war Ashford was made a reception area for evacuees from London, but by 1940 children were being evacuated away from the town to the safety of places like Oxford.

The Railway Works employed large numbers of women for the manufacture of essential war materials, and the town was fortified against the threat of invasion. Part of the Battle of Britain was fought in the skies above the town and it was included in what was to become known as 'Doodle-Bug Alley'.

Records show that 103 civilians were killed in the town with 162 seriously injured and another 245 received wounds that needed attention. The town had the unenviable record of having the highest single death toll in Kent from a single raid when 50 were killed in a three-minute attack by bombs and machine guns that strafed the streets and exploded on buildings. The rail works, always a regular target, Haywards Garage in New Street, and homes and businesses on Dover Place, New Rents, Hardinge and Star Roads, and Kent Avenue were all badly damaged in the raid.

Inside the old Corner Exchange traders discuss seed deals in this 1963 picture. The building was demolished and replaced by an office block for the Commercial Union Assurance and shops on the corner of Bank Street and Elwick Road.

Throughout the years the main feature on the low hill on which Ashford stands, was the parish church of St Mary with its 120 feet bell tower with pinnacles and clock which was a landmark for miles around.

Today it vies for position on the sky-line with the three-winged post-war office block known as Charter House which is the most noticeable building and greatest in size in the town centre which still has its early narrow streets and buildings from around 1500 in Middle Row. It is easy to criticise those in power but the preservation of this area and that around the ancient churchyard is greatly to the credit of those who make such decisions.

But on the outskirts of town housing and light industrial estates grew rapidly and the pace of change was accelerating after the war when the development explosion started.

In the late 1940s both the Twelve Acres estate at Willesborough with 208 homes and Woolreeds in south Ashford with 462 were opened, and work

opportunities were widening with the Norman Cycle Works in major new workshops in Beaver Road, from where a decade later they were producing over 5,000 bicycles, 600 mopeds and 120 motor cycles a week.

The 1950s were another decade of vast progress. The railway works produced their first diesel locomotive and new schools opened at Willesborough, Beaver Green and Stanhope.

The housing boom continued with the completion of the Musgrove estate in south Ashford, quickly followed by the Repton housing project of 138 houses; the Burton estate at Kennington (164); Aylesford Green, Willesborough (48) and Beaver Green, south Ashford (93 plus shops).

Expanding population brought pressure on the roads and the town centre often ground to a halt due to the sheer weight of traffic attempting to pass through the narrow streets. It was a relief to everyone when Ashford by-pass was completed and opened by Minister of Transport Harold Watkinson in 1957.

The official opening of Ashford bypass was recorded with great pomp and ceremony in 1957.

The town was planning for a vibrant future and the new Ashford Grammar School was opened in Hythe Road by The Earl Mountbatten of Burma in 1958 allowing the old school buildings to be taken over by the North Boys School.

The following year saw the opening by Sir Edward Hardy of the new £25,000 fire brigade headquarters at Bybrook, Kennington; and the start of the Church of St Francis of Assisi that opened to serve the new developments around Cyrol Road, South Ashford.

But without doubt the most significant date of the decade was the signing of the London overspill agreement to build 4,250 homes, the vast proportion of which were on what was to become the Stanhope estate.

The swinging sixties saw the sudden closure of the Norman Cycle Works, but there was no let-up in the pace of progress. The population was exploding and

new senior schools – Duncan Bowen at Stanhope and the Towers Secondary School at Kennington – were opened.

This was the decade when electric train services began to operate from Ashford, and familiar buildings began to be lost in the town centre. The Salvation Army's Norwood Street Chapel was demolished to make way for the new police headquarters; the new telephone exchange opened in Regents Place; and Ashford Library was opened in Church Road by Sir Kenneth Clark.

Grosvenor Hall at Kennington was taken over by the Metropolitan police as a cadet training college and the Intelligence Corps came to Templar Barracks.

Furley Hall, the new headquarters of Ashford St John Ambulance Brigade at Barrow Hill, was opened by HRH Princess Margaret as Commandant-in-Chief of the Ambulance and Nursing Cadets. The same day

An early view of Ashford's first shopping centre when cars could still park at one of the main entrances to load their buys in the days before town centre pedestrianisation.

The town lost many familiar buildings in the name of progress. The Congregational Church on the corner of Church Road and Tufton Street was demolished to make way for new law courts. The old Elwick Club for gentlemen in Tufton Street was pulled down as part of the Tufton Centre Shopping Centre, which was later renamed County Square, but shortly afterwards a splendid new £225,000 club was developed opposite the new library in Church Road ...to which female members were later admitted!

This was a time when many long-serving shops were lost to the town. The Lewis & Hyland store and other shops in New Rents and the Upper High Street were also demolished to make way for the Tufton Centre, and after 128 years service Headley's retail shop at 46 High Street ceased trading.

Royal visits to town were increasing and ever popular with the community. HRH Princess Margaret visited Letraset one of the highly-successful companies on the Kingsnorth Industrial estate; and HM The Queen led members of the Royal family in celebrations to mark the 500th anniversary of Ashford Parish Church in 1970.

In 1975 the Stour Centre Sports and Leisure Complex opened in Tannery Lane and three years later the William Harvey Hospital first opened its doors to out-patients. Ashford Grammar School changed its name to The Norton Knatchbull School in 1973 and Downs View Infants school opened in Kennington in 1976.

she opened the new Brake Hall building at Ashford School in East Hill.

When Lord Brabourne was president of the 100th Ashford Fat Stock Show at the Cattle Market HRH Prince Philip, the Duke of Edinburgh awarded prizes to the winners.

The 1970s was another decade of spectacular progress not least with the Grant of Arms which officially marked Ashford's status as a borough in 1976 two years after the amalgamation of Ashford urban district with East and West Ashford and Tenterden rural, and Tenterden borough councils.

A serious fire gutted the old Provender Flour Mill in East Hill, but the skills of the fire officers saved the seven-storey block at its centre, and it was later converted into the districts first night club complex.

The Intelligence Corps received the Freedom of the Borough in 1979 with Mayor, Major Bill Cotton presenting the casket to Sir Michael Gow, Colonel-Commandant of the Corps. To mark the Queen's Silver Jubilee year in 1977 the Harper

When Kennington got its first secondary school in 1967 it was a cause for major celebration. Here the first headmaster, Geoffrey Foster (standing centre), poses for pictures with the founding staff.

Crowds gathered in 1973 to watch a cavalcade of vehicles to mark the opening of Ashford by-pass which brought relief to the traffic-choked town centre.

Fountain in Victoria Park was restored to working order by the council with financial support from local business.

Times had been tough in the rundown of the railways but the wagon department at the Rail Works proudly announced in 1974 the building of 20 wagons for Yugoslavian Railways worth £6.5 million. This was hailed as the first of many major export orders for the area, but just seven years later British Rail announced the closure of the works due to dwindling export orders and cutting back on UK rolling stock. It forced the loss of almost 1,000 jobs and was a major blow to the town.

But the decade of the 1980s had started with much promise. No one worried about a Channel Tunnel because few guessed that the project cancelled midstream in 1975 would be revived. As the decade progressed and the prospect of its imminent arrival outside Folkestone got closer, it became a conversational bore.

No one had yet dreamed of a High-Speed Rail Link, they were still awaiting the completion of the M20 Motorway between Ashford and Maidstone that was considered the most vital missing link holding back progress towards prosperity of the district.

Few had visions of the green fields on Ashford's fringes as development sites suggested for Sevington and Kingsnorth. The public was unaware that Trinity College owned large tracts of Kennington and would win the right to convert 80 acres into a high-tech science and business park – now known as Eureka.

In the early 1980s visitors could take their pick of

December 1976 and construction work is almost complete on both the access road bridge over the river and the Stour Leisure Centre in Tannery Lane.

The linking of Ashford to the national motorway network, by completing the long-awaited M20 section from Maidstone, was a cause for major celebration. Before the official opening thousands strolled on the high-speed carriageways, some rode by horse and trap, and the Smith, Cadogan and Gammon families from Willesborough and Braboume held a picnic in the fast lane.

vacant rooms in and around town, but those in the hotel trade were all preparing for expansion convinced that supply would quickly be outstripped by demand for facilities.

The Post House planned to double capacity, The Holiday Inn built a 100 room hotel at Hothfield on the old Kempton Manor site, and Ashford International developed 200 plus luxury rooms at their hotel on the edge of town. Many more major hotel chains, including the Hilton, were reported to be looking for sites in the area.

This was the decade when Ashford ended its long tradition as a railway-engineering town – and then reclaimed its role in railway history by being chosen as the location for the International Passenger Station on the Channel Tunnel route. The new future beckoned with the airport-style station and its rapid services to Paris, Lille and Brussels that quickly attracted the imagination of European minded business.

Ashford, of course, already had strong European links of friendship, for more than a quarter of a century with the Germans from the Rhineland town of Bad Munstereifel, and for a decade with the Brittany community of Fougeres. Those continental connections are marked by the Friendship Stone, an irregular column of basalt that proudly stands in the Lower High Street. In 1981 those links were being celebrated again when German Burgermeister Heinz Gerlach opened a new £638,000 complex of 31 flats

for elderly people named after him in Beecholme Drive, Kennington.

These were also the infant days of the Julie Rose 10 kilometre road race and fun runs set up as a tribute to the young local athlete killed in a United States air crash. Her enthusiasm and need to go to America to get suitable training facilities inspired many to support the creation and development of an athletic stadium that was immediately the envy of southern England.

Norton Knatchbull School marked its 350th anniversary in 1980 with HRH Prince Charles, the Prince of Wales opening a new sports pavilion; in 1983 the new £4 million Civic Centre with pagoda-style roof, overlooking the River Stour in Tannery

The Cinema in Beaver Road was demolished in January 1992 to make way for the new roundabout and access road outside Ashford International Passenger Station.

Lane, was opened by HRH the Duchess of Kent; and the Bishop of Southwark, Michael Bowen opened the £600,000 St Therese's Roman Catholic primary school for 231 pupils in Quantock Drive in 1984.

This was also the year when Ashford lost another famous landmark when the Victoria Road flour mills of Messrs H.S. Pledge & Sons was gutted by a fire of catastrophic proportions which required the complete demolition of the site which was constructed in 1890.

Ashford town centre, thanks to the boldness and speculation of traders, the Chamber of Commerce and Industry and the borough council, was striving to make a name as an attractive shopping centre to serve an ever growing and demanding local community. They quickly accepted that it had to be different in style from the mass produced commercial efforts of Canterbury and Maidstone with whom it was

accepted Ashford would not seek to either copy or compete against.

It was in this decade that they could point with pride to the development of the Park Mall Shopping Centre, the first efforts to revitalise the High Street and the award winning multi-million pound upgrading of County Square.

Pedestrian-only precincts had arrived with attendant one-way streets, parking regulations, taxi driver protests and shopkeeper whinges about lost trade. It was a time of major change. Even the cattle market, a fixture in Ashford history since earliest times, was talking of vacating its Elwick Road setting, to make way for more shops and walkways over to link with the new station. That plan, like so many others never materialised, but the market transfer to distant Sevington was to be completed to make space for the rail line expansion.

Many had moaned about the conversion of the High Street Odeon cinema into a bingo hall, but there appeared to have been no major protests when the last remaining picture house, The cinema in Beaver Road, was surrendered to new road works associated with the international rail station; although the debate about the need for a replacement was a talking point for years after the loss.

Ashford Town Football Club was also on the move. It quit its home since before the war at Essella Park that became another housing estate, for a new out-of-town site called Homelands at Kingsnorth.

No discussion about life would be complete without comment on the climate we endure and this decade brought fashionable talk of global warming and ozone layers home to the ordinary men and women's understanding. There were indeed some odd happenings on the weather front.

Many will still remember the severe snowstorms which brought the area to a standstill in January 1987, followed by the terrifying killer gales of the Great Storm in October the same year. Then came the long hot summer of 1989 with the drought of which we all thought was only in the memories of octogenarians.

Origins

ASHFORD dates from well before the Norman Conquest and has been an important market centre since the 12th century. It has a long and rich history but no one can be quite certain when the town was actually founded.

A Roman road, which ran through Ashford, was built to transport iron ore from the Weald of Kent to the Kent coast, but although some Roman remains have been found in and around the town, there is not enough evidence to suggest a settlement.

It is however possible that a small community could have stayed from time to time as Ashford was just a one day march away from Hythe, Canterbury and Faversham along the road route which roughly followed Kingsnorth and Beaver Roads in south Ashford and up Station Road and Wellesley Road through the town towards Kennington.

Some have suggested that the real origins of the town were in the 9th century at the time of the Viking invasion when Great Chart and Wye were the main settlements in the area. As the Vikings plundered these communities the inhabitants fled to the surrounding forests and many settled in a clearing on high ground, which was believed to have been in the vicinity of Barrow Hill, Ashford.

For several centuries this area was known as Esshetesford and historians differ in opinion over the origin of the name. Some suggest it indicates a ford over the river Eshe, which was the ancient name for the tributary of the River Stour which rises in Lenham; while others believed it stood simply for ash trees growing near a ford.

Prior to the Norman invasion, it is recorded that part of Ashford was owned by St Augustine's Abbey at Canterbury, part belonged to King Edward the Confessor, and part to Earl Godwin, the father of Harold. After the Conquest St Augustine's retained its possessions, but the remainder was presented to Conqueror Commander Hugh de Montfort as reward for his services in battle.

Whatever the origins of the town or its name there can be no doubt that Ashford was established in 1085, the year King William the Conqueror ordered the making of the Domesday Survey. In that book compiled by the Normans there are clear references to the town having a church and two mills.

Four Manors of Ashford were described in Domesday. Ashford manor included all the town area, north to Bybrook, east to Willesborough, south to Beaver Lane, and west to Barrow Hill. Little and Great Repton Manor included lands to the north of the town; East Stour, the area later used for the railway works and northwards towards Hythe Road; and Wall which was a small manor in the area of Chart Leacon.

Because of its location Ashford has always played an important role in serving the farmlands that surround it, but it was not until the 13th century that the town was allowed a weekly market. Then fair and market rights were granted to Simon de Cryol in 1243 by Henry III – the market to be held every Saturday, and the fairs annually on 28, 29 and 30 August.

Royal Charters were granted for additional fairs in 1348 and 1466 and they continued until 1671 when Philip, Viscount Strangford who was then Lord of the Manor of Ashford, was empowered to hold a market on every other Tuesday for the selling of beasts and other merchandise.

The market held in the 120 feet wide lower High Street quickly grew in importance as roads improved and foot, packhorse and some wheeled transport brought in livestock. It continued until 1856 but there were increasing problems as the volume of trade improved much to the annoyance of those not involved in market business.

With concern growing a meeting of local farmers and graziers with Robert Furley, Clerk to the Justices of the Peace, and chaired by James Amos, was held in January 1856. A month later, following a public meeting at the Saracen's Head hotel, the Ashford Cattle Market Company Limited was formed with capital of £2,500.

A five-acre site in Elwick Road was leased from Lord of the Manor George Jemmett for 99 years, and he also sold all the market rights of the manor. The Market Company exercised their right to purchase the site in 1868 and the trade has continued until very recent times.

The new site was first used for the traditional May Fair and the official opening of the first general market was on 29 July 1856 after which a commemoration dinner, chaired by a Mr Harvey of Godmersham, was held for 250 people in the High Street Assembly Rooms.

From the start the market was an outstanding success and further expansion was needed to support the farming industry. The practice of selling corn by sample, rather than in bulk, was well established by the 19th century. Ashford had two rival areas for dealing, which was done in both the Royal Oak pub and the public rooms in Middle Row.

Increased demand for space led to proposals for a new base and a company was formed and by 1861 the new Corn Exchange was built and opened at the lower end of Bank Street, right opposite the cattle market. Built of brick with a roof of cast iron and glass the main room was 100 feet long and 35 feet high and there was seating for 1,000 people. The grand opening banquet was presided over by Sir Norton J. Knatchbull.

The building quickly became the centre for all manner of public entertainment and exhibitions until much to the dismay of many it was demolished in the 1970s and replaced by an office block.

The Parish Church of St Mary the Virgin is built of Kentish ragstone in early and late decorated perpendicular styles. It is likely that in the four centuries that followed the Norman invasion, the Saxon church mentioned in the Domesday Book was enlarged or completely rebuilt.

Parts of the church date back to the 13th century, but it was substantially restored including building a new tower, by Sir John Fogge, Lord of Repton Manor

between 1415 and 1483, who was one of the town's most celebrated benefactors.

Sir John, who was Comptroller and Keeper of the Wardrobe to Henry VI, Treasurer to the Household of Edward IV, Sheriff of Kent, and represented Kent in Parliament, also founded a College of Priests in the town in 1461. This was later disestablished but the timber-framed college now still forms part of the Vicarage and can been seen from the churchyard.

Many further alterations have been made since his death in 1490. In 1616 galleries were erected in the church and a few years later more were added for the use of the Grammar School based in the adjacent building, known today as the Dr Wilks Memorial Hall and home of Ashford Museum. In 1620 a peal of bells was hung in the tower and in 1688 a clock was installed with one large clockface on the north side. Then there were few buildings south of the church and it was not until it was replaced in 1885 that faces appeared on both the north and south side of the tower.

The first Ashford Grammar School was founded by Sir Norton Knatchbull of Mersham-le-Hatch in 1630 in the churchyard building where a master was employed at £30 per annum and he was required to have a Master of Arts degree, while to become a pupil boys had to be able to read the Old and New Testaments. Latin and Greek were taught free but there were fees for learning English and French.

The school remained in constant use until it moved to Hythe Road in 1876 and expanded considerably. In the final decade in the heart of the town records show that the roll of pupils was a dozen day boys aged between ten and 14 years plus 13 boarders who lived in the Headmaster's house in the High Street.

Ashford was also not totally unaffected by many of the main events in history through the centuries and a number of local people played prominent roles. The rebellion of 1450, against the corrupt administration and heavy taxes imposed by King Henry IV, started in Kent and was led by Jack Cade.

The revolt was directed against Royal advisers because they were held responsible for the state of affairs, and he led a body of 20,000 men of Kent in a march to Penenden Heath in Maidstone. Many of the

An early view of East Hill when it was still the main route taking all the traffic to Willesborough and the coast.

At the turn of the century, drovers brought thousands of sheep to market through the narrow streets, as seen here with two flocks about to enter from Elwick Road.

The exact date is unknown but this shows a typical scene at one of the early cattle market days on the Elwick Road site.

locals look part in the uprising were later pardoned but Cade was captured and killed at Hothfield.

In the 16th century it was religion rather than economics that was the cause of local discontent, and in Henry VIII's reign, John Brown, a heretic who was denounced by Archbishop Wareham, was burnt at the stake in the Martyr's Field at the bottom of East Hill on Whit Sunday in 1511. He stood accused of heresy for his lack of belief in the theory that priests were invested with certain supernatural powers when ordained.

In 1553 many locals supported Thomas Wyatt of Allington who led an attempt to overthrow the Catholic Queen Mary who had succeeded her brother Edward VI on the throne, but many had to flee abroad when the rebellion failed. Those that were caught were burnt alive as heretics whether they be men, women or children. It was usual for these executions to be carried out away from the home of the condemned to reduce the possibility of supporters attempting an escape.

At least five men from Ashford were all burnt at Canterbury and two men from Tenterden, Nicholas Final and Matthew Bradbridge, were burnt together at the stake in the Martyr's Field beside Hythe Road.

There was, however, a remarkable escape for Richard Brown whose father had died by fire in Ashford 41 years earlier. He was in Canterbury prison awaiting his own death by burning sentence but was saved by the death of the Queen in 1558.

The original Ashford stock market was held in the lower High Street, as is shown in this drawing by George Shepherd.

The Pump in Ashford High Street, pictured here in 1903, was in fact a handsome drinking fountain, built on the site of the old town pump, which was erected and given to Ashford by local historian and solicitor Robert Furley.

Handcarts parked at the junction of High Street and East Hill around the turn of the century.

Locals pose for the camera in New Street, Ashford in the early years of the 20th century.

Established in 1750, Rabson's toy store in Middle Row at the entrance to the churchyard was a delight to generations of youngsters until the 1970s.

This ancient building in Middle Row has seen a wide variety of uses over the centuries when it has served as the base for a printers, a lock-up for local criminals and as Ashford's first coffee bar in the 1950s.

The rear of Middle Row homes facing the north side of the churchyard included the popular Passmore's Restaurant.

Still clearly recognisable is The Blacksmith's Arms, Lacton, now better known as The Street, Willesborough. The building has changed little but the road surface and transport to get a well-deserved pint of beer has improved dramatically over the years.

North Willesborough Post Office in Hythe Road looking towards Ashford centre early in the century. Run by a Mr Salmon, the business also served a grocers, millers and corn merchants. In recent years it has been a do-it-yourself shop and is now Dickinson's Windmill Cafe.

An early car parked at the top of Bank Street in the days when horse-drawn vehicles and bicycles were still the main form of transport.

Bridge House, now part of Ashford School in East Hill, was used for some time as a Military Rest Centre.

Until the re-design of the town centre, corn merchants Denne & Sons in North Street was still an important stopping post for farmers on market day.

The Fifty Shilling Tailors were one of the first national chain stores in town where business was brisk on the prime site at the corner of North Street and the High Street.

The Bandstand in Victoria Park was a major centre of outdoor entertainment attracting large crowds for concerts.

For generations the Saracen's Head Hotel on the corner of the High Street and North Street was the top social meeting place for business and commerce.

King's Parade looking west shows Ruffle Bros the hatters and tailors, Worgers, and Lloyds Bank on the corner of Bank Street.

Before the War

FROM the turn of the century until the start of World War Two many developments were taking place in the town that laid the firm foundations for its modern day future.

As the new Millennium dawned Ashford urban council was preparing to take over responsibility of the Burial Board which had established and opened a cemetery in Canterbury Road in 1859. That had replaced the half-acre site in Station Road, which rapidly filled and was later to be converted to a memorial garden. Canterbury Road was quickly running out of grave space and a decision was taken to acquire the 22-acre burial ground at Bybrook.

It was one of a number of schemes implemented by the new local authority to improve the town and its facilities. Others included a water tower at Barrow Hill in 1898 and in 1901 new wells and reservoir with a capacity of 280,000 gallons at Henwood. Electric power came to the town in 1926 and was used for the first time when the Duke of York came to open the new hospital in Kings Avenue.

In the first decade of the century business was steadily developing in several key areas. Quality printing with the most modern machinery was gaining the town a reputation which others envied. Headley Brothers, renamed at this time Invicta Press, expanded into large premises in Edinburgh Road, which were later to become the home of Hollington Prep School,

They became only the third firm of printers in Europe to install a Monotype printing press, which since has been universally used in quality book production. Six years later the site was destroyed by a fire, which caused £20,000 damage in just one hour. But the company re-built the business at the new works in Lower Queens Road, which is still their home.

Walter Geering opened his printing business from a small hired shed in Blue Line Lane that ran from Magazine Road to Park Street. In 1910 Mr Geering acquired the photographic and picture frame shops at 95 High Street, later demolished for the Tufton Centre entrance, and 83 High Street, and by 1932 the growth of Geerings saw the new printing works built.

H.S. Pledge and Sons completed major extensions to the East Hill Mill including the seven storey central block, and the Chamber of Commerce was formed with a Mr N.G. Hancock elected the first President.

There was considerable joy in Kennington when Mid Kent laid the first water supply in 1905 and the Corn Exchange, a favourite meeting place for entertainment during several generations, was refurbished with an added stage and dressing rooms to serve the 1,200 seat main hall.

Education facilities made major progress with the opening of Ashford Grammar School for Girls beside Maidstone Road and the County School for Girls in Marsh Street (which is now Station Road) as a Higher Education Secondary School with places for 90 pupils, both in 1907.

Three years later saw the foundation of Ashford Modern School, later shortened to Ashford School in East Hill, and the public Elementary School for Boys was built in Willesborough for 200 pupils in 1912.

Later the Central Schools opened in Beaver in 1931 and in 1933 the Essella Road Central Schools were opened and the British School in West Street closed with the pupils relocated to the new facilities. The West Street building was converted to become the headquarters of the Salvation Army.

Bicycle production in 1907 was beginning to gather pace in the district with Charles Hayward & Sons in New Street producing the quality 'Onward' machines with its inward lever rim brakes, plated rims and black enamel and gold finish, costing £8 10s (£8.50) each. Mr Hayward who had left his job in the rail works to go it alone had started the business in 1889.

It became a major production centre with a healthy export business until World War One when they switched to supporting the war effort and then continued through three generations as general and motor engineers on the Haywards Garage site with 6,000 square feet of workshops, later taken over by Caffyns, on either side of New Street.

The second great producer and major employers was the Norman Cycle Works, which had been founded in Castle Street by Charles Norman before World War One. He was later joined by his brother Fred and they became the major national suppliers of transport perhaps the most famous of which was the Norman Nippy moped.

They had major works in Victoria Road until 1934 when a large factory was built on a 34-acre site in Beaver Road. With 100,000 square feet of production area, thousands of cycles, motorbikes and mopeds were sold every week until the works closed quite suddenly in the 1960s.

This also the age of the cinema and saw the opening of Ashford's Electric Picture Palace in Tufton Street, on the present site of Courts Furniture Store. Plans had been formulated over two years for moving picture shows to be screened twice weekly in the Norwood Street Drill Hall. When the Picture Palace opened in 1911 Ashford was one of the few towns in Kent with a cinema – but without electricity.

The following year the Royal Cinema Deluxe opened in Beaver Road. Best seats in the house were one shilling (5p) and the cheapest three old pence. Before World War Two the classic Odeon Cinema opened in the lower High Street to make Ashford one of the best served areas for the showing of filmed entertainment.

Other areas for pastime and entertainment were also developing. A working men's club opened in Bank Street in 1922 and moved to its present site in Station Road four years later.

The first public library opened in Station Road and The Drill Hall and Territorial Headquarters in New-town Road were built and later used as the Post Office Sorting Office until they were demolished for road access to the International Passenger Station. Both the Conservative Institute at Willesborough and the Technical Institute in Elwick Road were opened in 1914.

During these early years residents attended a series of celebrations – some of joy but many in tribute to the memory of the loss of public figures. In 1910 to mark the death of King Edward VII, who had been a frequent visitor to Ashford during his many stays at Eastwell Manor, an Arbor Day in Victoria Park saw the planting of 40 trees.

A major Industrial, Trade and Arts exhibition organised by Ashford Chamber of Commerce was held in Ashford Market in 1911 in honour of the coronation of King George V and Queen Mary.

The big news of 1912 was the sinking of the *Titanic* and the loss of more than 1,500 passengers and crew one of which was 24-year-old steward Bernard Boughton of Hardinge Road. A special service was held in Victoria Park in memory of all victims and a collection of £50 was taken to help survivors.

Two years later at St Mary's Church a memorial service was held to honour the loss of Lord Kitchener who was lost at sea when his ship sunk en route to Russia. The following year it was the sinking of the *Glenart Castle* that left parishioners mourning the loss of St Mary's curate the Rev F.H. Edinger who had been ship's chaplain in these times of war.

The war impact on Ashford was limited to a small number of air raids. In August 1915 a Zeppelin airship dropped incendiary and explosive bombs on Queen's Road and The Warren without injuries, but a daylight aircraft raid in 1917 killed one person in South Ashford.

To mark the end of the war there were unprecedented scenes of rejoicing on the streets with all-clear sirens sounding and church bells ringing. There were parades through streets decked out with flags and bunting and effigies of The Kaiser were burnt to celebrate the end of World War One.

In 1920 the War Memorial Gardens, for centuries Glebe Land of the parish church between Station and Church Roads, were presented to the urban council and three years later the stone cross war memorial was erected to honour those from the town that died in foreign fields. Earlier a rood screen had been erected in Ashford Parish Church to remember those that had fallen in service during the battles.

Between the two world wars expansion and development continued with the council acquiring The Warren as an area of open space of major importance, and for the first time the parishes of both Kennington and Willesborough were included in the urban district.

The Coronation Day parade through Ashford High Street in 1911.

The Royal Cinema de Luxe which opened in Beaver Road in 1912.

Ashford Telegraph Messengers team who were winners of the Ashford District Football League in both 1903 and 1904.

Ashford Wanderers Cricket Club touring side from the summer of 1913.

Caxton House cricket team pose for a group picture in 1914.

Staff of the British School in West Street pictured shortly before World War One.

The 1st Ashford Scouts helped with the billeting of soldiers in 1915. This early picture shows them using the camping trekcart to move the kitbags in the foreground.

Kitchener's Army on parade in Ashford in 1915, on the march in Bank Street between the Corn Exchange and the Market Hotel.

The Memorial Gardens were presented to the town in 1920 with the stone cross war memorial erected three years later to honour those lost in conflict.

The Rev Alfred Turner, minister of Ashford Congregational Church between 1853 until 1895, raised funds to start the British School, which was based in West Street until 1928. This class picture, taken in 1922 or 1923, includes headmaster Mr Cole and teacher Miss Moffett.

Staff and pupils, including a youthful Joe Fagg, of Ashford Central School in Victoria Road, in 1926. The school opened two years earlier and remained at the site until 1932. It was a new style school for Ashford with boys attending from both the town and villages after passing an entrance exam. Students were able to continue education until the age of 15. When the South Modern School was built in Jemmett Road, headmaster Mr Humphreys, the teachers and boys all moved to the larger premises.

South Willesborough Boy Scouts' band in 1927.

The pre-war Mersham football team pictured at their headquarters field when it was located near the A20 turning into the village. The 1928-29 season team pictured here included Arch Griggs, Jack Pilbeam, Les Foster, Tommy Ruck and Cyril Griggs.

Middle Row in 1926 when Dixon's ironmongers stood for almost a century in a building that was later converted to an extension for the present Man of Kent pub.

A rare picture of the butcher's shop in Upper Denmark Road, Ashford, run by Frank and Win Brown. Hygiene laws were more lax with the meat always hanging outside the shop, including this selection, prepared for the Christmas Market Show of 1931, being displayed by the owners and staff.

The bottom end of Bank Street towards the junction with Elwick Road, pictured between the wars.

In the 1930s many wives of local traders were leading members of Ashford Townswomen's Guild which met regularly at the Masonic Hall in North Street. Pictured here is the line-up for the annual fund-raising garden party, which included a musical entertainment, called *The Cries of London*.

Shortly before the outbreak of war, the girls of Beaver Road Junior School pose for a 1939 picture. Back row (left to right): Margaret Smail, Joyce Rave, Joan Harding, Dorothy Luckhurst, Peggy Roach. Middle: Pat Dixon, Kath Robinson, Audrey Laker, Winnie Kay, Pat Howard, Pamela Gooding, Joan Edwards, Betty Chittenden. Front: June Taylor, Betty Randall, Betty Bamen, Daisy Roots, Jennie Roberts, Daisy Gutteridge, Irene Gower, Peggy Luckhurst, Betty Chapman and June Morris.

The Rail Works

ASHFORD has 150 years of railway industry to look back on with pride. That journey from the age of steam to the speed of Eurostar all started in November 1842 on Ashford Railway station.

People travelled from the surrounding areas by horseback, cart and on foot to enjoy the spectacle and witness the coming of the railway to town.

Some objected to the noise, and because it clashed with their own financial interests, but most were vocal in their support. The track was laid and everyone made the most of the festive occasion, which was supported by coloured bunting, and a big turnout of the town dignitaries.

The hiss and clatter and smells of steam loco-motion that persisted for generations were savoured by all in these pre-electric days. As the decades passed, Ashford quietly but quickly established itself as a centre of engineering excellence.

Then came the devastating announcement in 1981 that the railway works was to be run down and closed by June 1984 leaving many redundant after a lifetime of service. It was the biggest body blow in the modern history of the town.

The first rail services ran from London to Ashford via Redhill and were operated by South Eastern Railway. The following year the line was extended to Folkestone. In 1846 the branch to Canterbury was opened and five years later the line to Hastings.

Ashford Railway Works at Newtown were established in 1847 where the magnificent steam locomotives were constructed until 1936. Then they concentrated on repair work until World War Two when they were building both trains and providing support services to the forces.

In peace again high quality wagon production became the priority although there were major changes brought about by the advent of electri-fication in 1961.

Great efforts were made to boost exports and in 1973 the first oversees order for 800 wagons to go to Yugoslavia were completed with skill and dedication and on time to the highest standards. Further export orders followed to Kenya, Tanzania, Jordan, Israel and Bangladesh, but all these massive efforts proved to be too little too late to save the works.

It had all started when the directors of South Eastern Railway bought 185 acres of farmland for £21,000 to create a 'Locomotive Establishment'. From that moment progress in creating the famous Ashford Works was swift, although there were some protests along the way.

For instance it was reported that the Archbishop of Canterbury had expressed grave concern over the inadequacy of church provision for the large number of men to be employed. It is recorded that the rail company swiftly provided a grant of £100 towards the stipend of the Rev John Pughe to minister to the spiritual needs of the workforce.

By the following year 70 labourers' cottages were built and over the years a complete village of Alfred – now known as Newtown – was constructed with a school, general store, public baths and washing facilities, church and public house, the Alfred Arms, which still stands and serves the community.

By the end of 1851 the works were supporting a community of nearly 3,000 people including the wives and families of workers and the long building sheds were a hive of activity turning out the finest standard design locomotives.

James Cudworth was the first of the great engine designers of Ashford from 1853 when the works was fully operational with an impressive selection of massive workshops considered the most modern of the day. The main shed was almost 400 feet long and 64 feet wide with numerous other specialist shops providing engineering of the greatest precision.

It was at this time that the railway church of Christ Church, south Ashford, was build and dedicated with the costs almost entirely met by shareholders of the railway, although why it was not built on Newtown is something of a mystery.

Through the generations the works were to have a succession of brilliant award-winning designers and engineers which kept Ashford at the cutting edge of the railway industry.

During World War Two the works were to play an important role. Armour plating, mobile workshops, bomb-trolleys, ramp wagons for conveying tanks, and breakdown trains for the United States Army were just some of the essential war material to come from the Ashford workforce.

In the Klondike shops new goods wagons were being produced at the astounding rate of one every hour. In 1942 a record was created when 1,600 12-ton wagons needed for shipment to Persia were built in 12 weeks.

Ashford was the first depot in the nation to be equipped with light anti-aircraft guns, which were manned by their own staff Home Guard unit. They were a prime target for the German bombing raids and there were six major hits and a number of deaths, but they never managed to cause a major breakdown in either spirit or production.

By 1947 the centenary of the works saw major efforts being made to both make good the destruction of war and to overcome the problems of post-war material shortages.

But they still managed to record 715 new locomotives built during the year and another 300 re-built. The carriage department was also producing an average of 55 wagons in every 55-hour week.

At this time the works had 156 apprentices learning their trades in the workshops and its own team of 120 trained Ambulance men. It was a massive self-sufficient operation that cared with a passion for the staff, even providing a full range of sporting facilities ranging from bowls to tennis and cricket facilities for workers.

The switch from steam to diesel and quickly to electric clearly ended the need for many of the wide range of heavy skills practised to perfection in the works, but it was still a major shock to the town when the closure notice was posted.

But the town has survived and railways continue to be a vital part in both the present and future of the district. The major changes of 1961 which brought electrification saw the establishment of the Chart Leacon Repair Shop which continues to thrive under new ownership, but still using the skills of local railwaymen.

Eurostar has arrived with its high-speed services to the continent and the ultra-modern Ashford International Passenger Station is the envy of many. And probably the biggest railway project yet still has to come with the construction of the high-speed link line to London from the coast.

Ashford seems certain to continue to be part of the next railway revolution.

Staff take time off to pose for a picture inside the busy railway works in 1906.

Workers clock-off after another long shift at Ashford railway works in 1913.

A fine view of Ashford railway works taken from Newtown Bridge in 1915.

Sir Patrick Spens, MP, was among the many VIPs to visit the railway works to praise the contribution of women volunteers during World War Two. Here he is pictured with bench-hand Mrs L. R. Hogben, who joined her husband who was a machinist in the same workshop.

A woman blacksmith happy in her job in the smith shop at Ashford railway works. Mrs Dorothy Stanford-Beale previously served in her father's fruiterer's shop.

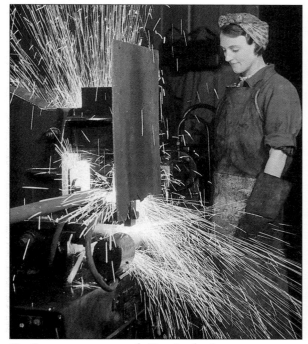

Caution – women at work. Despite the dangers numerous women took manual jobs in Ashford railway works in a major war effort.

Hold it still! This woman is no shirker, wielding a heavy hammer in the smithy as women did men's work.

This woman is cutting engine boiler tubes. Before the war she was in domestic service in Ashford.

Driving a small delivery truck – no matter what the job, women were ready to help the war effort.

These women are cleaning train lighting battery cells.

Her thoughts may be on a night out, or a weekend off, but for the moment this young lady is concentrating on operating a heavy machine.

Life in the engineering works was tough but extremely skilful with precision engineering that was the envy of many other production units.

In gleaming bottle-green paint and new brass work shining, Loco 737 was a reminder of the colourful days before nationalisation made all railway trains look alike. To say farewell to the old days in June 1960 were (from left to right) Mr F. Howard, retired Ashford motive power superintendent, Lt Colonel J. Bell, Ashford rail works manager, Mr L. Lynes, retired SE & Chatham Railway chief draughtsman, Mr K. Masters, Mr W. Covey, Loco Progress Inspector, Mr W. Howland, paint shop foreman, and Mr J. Finch, retired assistant works manager.

Newtown Bathhouse which was built in 1852 and served both the residents of Alfred Town and the rail workers.

The gatehouse, tower and clock at the entrance to Newtown railway works remains almost untouched by the passing years.

This was the site of the 'new' Ashford rail works being prepared at Chart Leacon in 1959 beside the Great Chart road. Workers removed 40,000 tons of earth from the 17-acre site before constructing the electrical repair and inspection sheds which provided work for 300 staff.

Ashford at War

MEMORIES are still vivid for all who lived through Ashford's six long years of war. For the most part they were ordinary people caught up in the extraordinary conflict, who wanted no more than to live their lives in peace.

Innocent residents were caught in the front-line of battles because of the town's location as a vital communications link and of the expertise of the railway works. It meant threats from the skies, almost daily bringing fears of death and destruction which was faced not only with remarkable courage, but often with much humour.

Statistics show that Ashford suffered the third greatest number of casualties in Kent after Dover and Canterbury. One hundred and three people died with 162 seriously injured and another 245 needed treatment to wounds.

In all, 184 properties were completely destroyed and another 393 homes and businesses damaged by enemy raiders who dropped 974 high explosive bombs, 12,645 incendiary bombs and 184 flying bombs on the district.

Ashford also had the unenviable record of the worst death toll from a single attack on any area in the county when 50 died in a three-minute raid on Wednesday, 24 March 1943.

A dozen Focke-Wulf 190s of the infamous JG54 squadron based at St Omer, led by one of Germany's leading pilots, Staffelkaptan Oberleutant Paul Keller, swooped over the town at roof-top height in three waves bombing and machine-gunning everything in their path. In addition to the deaths, another 77 people were seriously injured and 79 slightly hurt in the savage attack, but it could have been even worse as there was a remarkable story of narrow escape.

Three hundred youngsters, aged between eight and 11, were at lessons in the Victoria Road Primary School, when the warning sirens sounded. Such was their discipline and training that they were all packed into the playground shelters seconds before a bomb scored a direct hit on the school and two classrooms, where 80 girls had been moments earlier, were destroyed.

The children emerged from their shelters to find much of their school missing, and worried parents and friends who had rushed to the playground, which was covered in debris from the blasts, were amazed that every single child had escaped unhurt.

The fighter-bombers were first spotted approaching shortly after the warning siren went. Two observers on duty on top of Newtown Bath House saw the aircraft approaching out of the sun from the Mersham direction at less than 100 feet from the ground. Danger signals sounded and everyone in the rail works had just 25 seconds warning to find cover. Most reached safety but eight men from the massive workforce died and 41 were injured.

Five bombs dropped on the works including one on the erecting shed, which was so badly damaged that production was halted for three weeks. The power of the blast tossed 50-ton engines around like toys. Two bombs blasted the running-shed and one hit a steam locomotive and killed both the driver and the fireman.

Two people died at Haywards Garage in New Street which received a direct hit wrecking the buildings and stored cars, and igniting inflammable supplies, causing a massive blaze. It was one of a dozen fires blazing throughout the town and 25 fire engines had to be called in from out of town to bring them under control.

A baker, his wife and son and two workers were all killed when the Bakers Shop in Kent Avenue was hit. Milton Road was the worst hit by damage with seven homes destroyed and every other one badly damaged by the explosions.

Several children and animals escaped unhurt from the ruins throughout the town centre, but as rescue workers dug for trapped people in the rubble all day and throughout the night by floodlight, the death toll was rising.

A women of 90 and her housekeeper died in one home and a mother and her three-year-old daughter in another. It was a day and night of great mourning. Dover Place, New Rents, Star Road and Hardinge Road were all badly damaged by bombs and the rescuers supported by off duty soldiers and members of the Home Guard, checked every one for casualties, as members of the local WVS and Salvation Army kept everyone supplied with hot drinks and food.

In just three minutes more than 700 homes were damaged, many beyond repair, but for those who suffered there was some consolation when news reached them that the German air-ace leader had been shot down by anti-aircraft fire.

Keller, nicknamed the 'Bombenkeller of St Omer' had led something of a charmed life with his daring low-level raids in Kent and London that had inflicted major damage before his final destructive raid on Ashford.

His plane was hit by Ack-Ack fire and exploded in the skies above Godinton Road where it crashed in pieces. The engine caused some damage, but no injury to a home in the road, and Keller himself was thrown out of the craft in flames to land on the nearby playing field where he died before either arrest or rescue. Reports also indicate that a second of the raiders that day was destroyed and crashed into the Channel as it returned to the French base.

Just eight weeks earlier the first major attack of the year had seen four low-level enemy raiders strike at 8am. Prompted by increased activity by RAF Bomber Command over Germany this was one of the hit and run reprisals, which proved to be deadly effective.

The Focke-Wulf aircraft again came in at rooftop level for the dawn raid and in less than two minutes six were killed, 11 seriously injured and 15 more wounded as areas of St John's Lane, Birling Road and Penlee Point lay in ruins. Another bomb fell in the Co-op warehouse at the rear of the High Street where many windows were shattered.

With its involvement in vital war work the rail works was clearly a prime target in raids. Bombs had first fallen on the Newtown complex in July 1940 but

the first serious damage was not inflicted until October 1942 when a lone Dornier raider, under cover of low cloud, dropped two lunchtime bombs which killed ten men and a woman and badly damaged the heavy-machine shops.

Several of those killed had been sheltering beside a wall that blew in and collapsed on them when the bombs exploded. A month later two Focke-Wulf 190s attacked Ashford and killed one man in the works. Returning to France across Romney Marsh they spotted a train on the branch line to New Romney.

Driver and firemen with no protection cowered in the cab as the aircraft attacked. Bullets from the first hit the engine but missed the crew, but the second, flying low behind, clipped the steam dome on the locomotive and lost control. As it crashed into the marshes the pilot was thrown clear but drowned in a dyke. The engine driver escaped unhurt but his fireman needed hospital treatment for burns received from scalding steam from the ruptured engine.

War death first came to Ashford on 17 July 1940, when a single highflying raider dropped High explosive bombs on Newtown. One exploded in the works injuring several workmen, and others on Newtown green which wrecked a number of flats in which three were killed including a baby.

Newtown was again the target on 16 September when another two died in bomb blasts; and ten days later seven were killed in the town centre in a dive-bombing attack which badly damaged the area of Regents Place and East Street. One of the men who died received a direct hit on his car as he drove it into the Co-operative Yard in Godinton Road.

The skies above the district were alive with action on 15 September 1940, a date that will forever be known as Battle of Britain Day and a turning point in the war.

Those historic battles between the RAF heroes and the best the Luftwaffe could muster have been well recorded many times in words and film. Ashford celebrated like the rest of the country this turning point in Nazi Germany's failed bid to take our nation, but also mourned not only the flying heroes who died in the battle but the only civilian death in Kent on that memorable day.

It came when a German fighter crashed in flames

on a home in Bilsington killing one local. The house was destroyed and the force of the explosion also destroyed a nearby shop and scattered wreckage over a wide area.

For those people watching the dogfights from ground level it was almost impossible to identify the aircraft in action as they were diving and attacking in skies filled with tracers and smoke. But by midnight 61 enemy fighters and bombers had been shot down.

Some crashed into the sea as they attempted to limp back to their continental base, but the fields and villages of Kent were scattered with the burnt out remains of Messerschmitt 109s, Dorniers and Heinkels, including sites at Pluckley, Smarden, St Michael's, Tenterden, Lympne, Benenden, Sandhurst, and Hothfield. Hothfield was also the last resting-place of a Junkers 88 which was shot down and exploded on crashing on 1 September 1944 after attacking coastal shipping. This proved to be the last enemy aircraft to crash on Kentish soil.

Before the days of action, Ashford citizens, like all others, had faced the days known as the phoney peace and phoney war. Hitler was in power from 1933 and most thought that war was inevitable so steps were taken to increase training in first-aid and Observer Corps plane-spotters were preparing to alert the RAF with information about the enemy. Most were convinced that the war was to be won or lost in the air.

Air-raid precautions were regarded as top priority and in March 1938 Home Office Under Secretary of State, Geoffrey Lloyd, came to speak on this government policy at the Corn Exchange in Elwick Road. He reported that Kent had done generally well but that Ashford was lacking in public volunteer support.

Still Kent prepared for action in many ways with trial blackouts proving to be quite dangerous in themselves. A man of 74 was killed crossing the A20 road at Hothfield when he was knocked over by one car and then run over by another – both with masked headlights.

The phoney war ended in April 1940 and the first bombs to be dropped in England fell early on 10 May in fields at Petham and Chilham. Houses were shaken by the high explosives and the noise was heard in

Ashford although nobody was injured in this first raid.

The real war was about to start and the *Kentish Express* of 24 May told readers: 'People in Kent, especially in the south-eastern portion of the county, are living in a state of tenseness and excitement while fighting rages in France and Belgium and aircraft roar overhead. Gunfire and the bursting of bombs are heard unceasingly from the other side of the Channel, and anti-aircraft defences in this country. Since Saturday the sounds have been more intense, and some people claim to have heard machine-gun fire over the Channel'.

Kent was preparing for invasion and the beaches were protected with miles of barbed wire, concrete blocks and disguised gun emplacements. Convinced that paratroops and troop gliders would be in the first wave of landings all open spaces were ordered to be strewn with obstacles, which included numerous old vehicles.

Hitler's plan, codenamed Operation Sealion, was to attack Kent in landings between Folkestone and Romney Marsh after paratroops had dropped on the high ground above the marshes to secure crossings of the Royal Military Canal. They then planned to link with further waves of troops to form a bridgehead and hold a line from Ashford to Canterbury until further manpower arrived to launch the advance to capture much of Kent and Sussex.

Shortly before the planned invasion, four German spies who landed between Hythe and Dungeness were quickly captured showing that everyone was alert to the dangers.

It was around this time that a special secret army of civilians was being formed to harass the enemy if they were ever successful in landing in Kent.

The arms resistance fighters were fully trained and ready to wreak havoc. The man who formed the first guerrilla unit in Kent was Peter Fleming, a Grenadier Guards Captain, who was in fact brother of the creator of James Bond.

He was later replaced by Lt Col Norman Field whose hideaway headquarters was at Bilting close to the main Ashford to Canterbury road, yet tucked into the Downs on the edge of Challock Forest.

In great secrecy volunteers trained for expertise in

explosives and demolition, and indeed how to kill silently, in numerous countryside hideouts, including an enormous underground chamber in Godmersham Park, and others at Challock, Hastingleigh, Bethersden, Brookland, Tenterden, Rolvenden, Pluckley, Hawkhurst and Sutton Valence.

Had Hitler landed, this secret army would have worked in much the same way as the resistance movement in France. Although the threat of invasion diminished as the war developed, the volunteers continued to train twice a week until November 1944 when the 3,000 member strong Auxiliary Unit, as they were officially known, was stood down.

In the same year Field Marshall Bernard Montgomery, fresh from his victory in Alamein, was touring the south-east preparing for the allied invasion of France.

British troops were joined in increasing numbers by American soldiers and it was these GIs who were causing considerable interest in the local area. Everyone was intrigued by the brash attitude of over one million US soldiers nicknamed after the words 'Government Issue' on their equipment and the local girls in particular were impressed by their gifts of nylons and Lucky Strike cigarettes.

The threat of invasion still existed and the decision was taken to make Ashford a strongly defended garrison and tank-proof town.

In May 1941 Monty came to town, walked the boundary to confirm the perimeter of defence, and his orders to troops in this top-secret decision were crystal clear. The intention was that if invaded Ashford would hold out to the last against all attacks and there would be no withdrawal under any circumstances. The town was prepared to lay down lives for the nation.

Work started immediately to deepen the River Stour, into which Canadian soldiers placed pipes filled with high explosive, over a one-and-a-quarter mile stretch. This could be blown to create tank ditch barriers on invasion. At least three miles of concrete tank obstacles were placed, roadblocks constructed and an outer wire perimeter of almost five miles was laid.

Fortress Ashford had been established with a Captain G. M. Day of the 70th Buffs as Garrison Commander with headquarters at the town centre Vicarage. Quickly into position were 50 roadblocks, five rail blocks, 32 machine-gun and numerous anti-tank gun positions.

Within the town were 1,300 regular troops and 700 Home Guard, but despite all the preparations many civilians continued to live and work in the town unaware of the extent of plans for its defence.

Sector headquarters were established at Caxton House in Wellesley Road, Dover Place, Western Avenue and Magazine Road, with the Home Guard based at the Technical School in Elwick Road and the Post Office Home Guard in Tufton Street.

Ashford School in East Hill was taken over by the Royal Artillery, and a prisoner of war cage was constructed in Station Road, complete with an Interrogation Officer based in the adjacent Welfare Centre. Plans were in hand for all civilians not required to maintain essential services, to be evacuated immediately by rail if an invasion started, and from that moment Ashford would become a fortress town.

Not a minute was to be wasted once an attack was imminent and the call to action stations would see all wire gaps closed, roads blocked and mine fields laid. All petrol-pumps were to be sealed or destroyed and both road and rail petrol tankers overturned and punctured.

The flow of food into the town was to be halted and those inside, both military and civilian, would be fed either from Food Officer distribution under the Garrison Commander or in canteens provided by the civilian emergency committee.

Water was stored for emergency and allocated at two gallons a man to last a week and to be used only for drinking and cooking. There was no allowance made for washing and no water from any other source could be used without permission.

Casualties were expected to be high in the defence and a military medical officer was based at the Corn Exchange with 10 doctors, 43 nurses and more than 70 first-aid workers ready to be allocated to first-aid posts and dressing stations. Six civilian and one military ambulance were available to transport the wounded to emergency centres.

It was a major relief to everyone that by the

summer of 1942 threat of invasion all but disappeared, and the plans never had to be implemented.

It was also a time for the establishment of decoy airfields in which the Ashford district was to play a major role. In order to mislead the Luftwaffe, the Nazis were led to believe that the RAF was growing rapidly and that up to 50 squadrons were based in Kent.

Small airfields, to be known as advanced landing grounds, were constructed at Ashford, Kingsnorth, Egerton, High Halden, Woodchurch, Brenzett, New Romney, Newchurch and Headcorn. Each were to have dummy buildings and model aircraft and gliders in an elaborate plan of deceit to produce fake targets so convincing that the enemy would bomb them rather that the real airstrips.

For the most part it worked brilliantly but there were still some tragic deaths like the midnight raid two weeks before Operation Overlord, as the D-Day landings were known, when a 1,000 bomb fell on the tented RAF camp based in Coleman's Wood at Chilmington beside the Ashford airfield, killing eight men and seriously wounding another 16.

As the Allied invasion for the liberation of Europe got under way, Hitler was launching his latest orgy of terror on southern England in the form of the flying bomb or VI – more often known as the doodlebug.

The pilotless monoplanes of plywood and sheet metal each had a ton of explosive in its nose. Among the first killed on 17 June by this latest weapon were three people at Benenden, but one week later 47 soldiers died when a flying bomb crashed on Newlands Military Camp at Charing Heath. Another crashed on the village church at Little Chart and the impact brought down the walls. Nobody was injured but villagers campaigned to keep the ruins as a symbol of Kent's ordeal in that summer of 1944.

The slaughter continued with an estimated 8,000 doodlebugs launched over Kent in the 80 days before Allied troops reached the French launching sites.

In May the war in Europe was over and Ashford lost no time in celebrating peace with crowds gathering in Elwick Road and Bank Street at midnight to watch the burning of an effigy of Hitler which had hung from the Corn Exchange building.

Earlier people had danced in the town centre streets to music from the Southern Railway Works Band. The parish church, council offices and Willesborough windmill were all floodlit and the pubs kept open until 11.30pm.

Numerous celebration street parties were staged and around 1,000 people attended a special thanksgiving service at St Mary's Church.

Lines of tank obstacles and barbed wire dominated the outskirts of town as illustrated by these alongside the Maidstone road placed as part of the wartime defences.

Mersham village had its very own 'Dad's Army' group of uniformed Home Guard soldiers.

Women volunteers who were not in the Forces or nursing, willingly joined as Air Raid Precautions wardens. They did a man's job, and were proud of it, as this photograph taken at their Ashford post, clearly showed.

Like all other Kent towns, Ashford was constantly on the alert with many shop windows protected from bomb blasts. But everyday life continued, the shopping still had to be done, and there was a calm determination to get on with life, which is reflected by these housewives with full baskets crossing the High Street.

A car is blown on top of a baker's cart by a bomb blast in Victoria Road, Ashford, in September 1940.

Queen Victoria was not disturbed from her frame above the fireplace, but this was another Ashford home wrecked after a German raid in September 1940.

East Street was bombed on 26 September 1940, leaving many residents homeless and the road blocked.

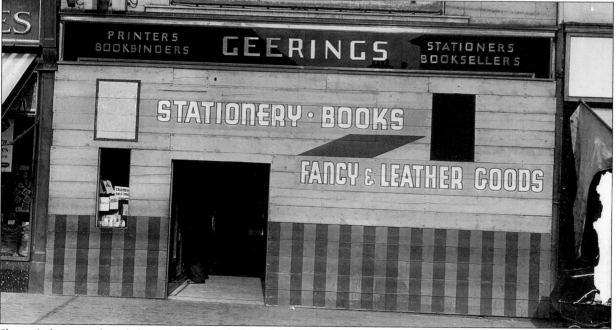

Shop windows were boarded up ready to stop the blast from bombs, but it was 'business at usual' at Geerings in Ashford High Street.

November 1940: Searching among the ruins for casualties following the bombing of the Church Road Library site.

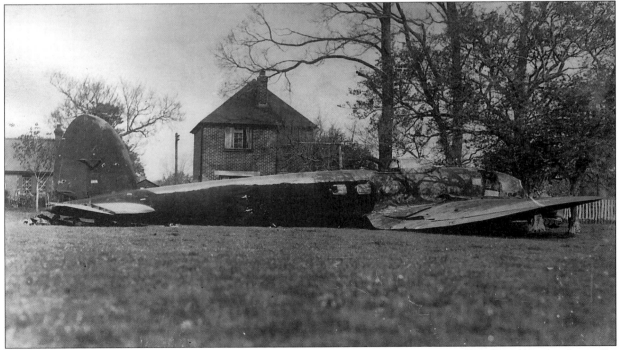

A German Heinkell 110 bomber shot down at Kennington in 1941. It is interesting to note that all markings and swastika signs were quickly blacked out on the wreckage.

The Duke of Kent inspects the local Home Guard units on a morale- boosting visit to Ashford on 3 May 1941.

The Duke of Kent also inspected members of the Wartime Civil Defence Service at Ashford during his May 1941 visit to the town.

Youngsters rescue the family chickens from the debris after another bombing attack on the town.

Three days before Christmas 1942, bombers destroyed these homes in Grosvenor Road, Kennington.

Soldiers helped with the rescue work after Snashell's Bakery in Kent Avenue was destroyed, killing seven people.

A daylight bombing raid in March 1943 damaged numerous vehicles and wrecked buildings in Dover Place as the Germans missed their target of the nearby railway station.

Hayward's Garage in New Street after the explosion in March 1943.

Ashford WVS continued to raise money during the war with this barrel organ providing the street entertainment in December 1943.

The Princess Royal took a particular interest in repairs being carried out by girl workers in the Ordnance Workshops in 1943.

The Princess Royal rode in a bren-gun carrier driven by a member of the ATS when she visited the REME Workshops in Chart Road.

Ashford's salute to the Armed Forces. Serviceman marched with pride through the lower High Street before vast crowds in July 1944.

Ashford High Street in September 1944 as work goes on to replace shattered street lamps.

Six GIs relax with local girls outside the American Red Cross Donut Dugout in the town centre.

Flags fly and happy faces returned at the many Ashford street parties in May 1945, held to celebrate VE Day.

Local Government

ASHFORD today is a thriving centre for business, industry and tourism and rightly heralded as Britain's Gateway to Europe. Many factors have helped to shape the future but much of the credit must be given to those in local government in the 1950s who launched long-term plans to encourage wide ranging job opportunities and build a strong and sustainable economic base.

The Urban District Council was formed in 1894 and, with the later addition of the parishes of Kennington and Willesborough in 1934, ruled the town for 80 years.

Then, as a result of the Local Government Act of 1972, the council was vastly expanded and merged with four others – East and West Ashford and Tenterden rural districts and Tenterden Borough Council.

Elected members were increased from 24 to 49 to form the present Borough in 1974 covering an area of about 144,000 acres and serving a population creeping towards 100,000. It remains the largest in area of the 14 districts in Kent.

It was the most dramatic change in rule and town clashed with country in establishing the development strategy of the new authority, after its Grant of Arms was presented on behalf of the Queen by Lord Lieutenant, Lord Astor of Hever.

But survive and prosper it quickly did – although not everyone appreciated the aims to progress from quiet country market town to vibrant business hub of East Kent.

A determination to succeed was quickly established between urban and rural members and, supported by officers with vision, Ashford set about capitalising on its strategic importance. They knew that geographical position had been a dominant factor in the town's history and were convinced that it was likely to shape its future.

It was quickly identified as an area of investment opportunity. Eventually the opening of the Channel Tunnel and even more vital the International Passenger Station highlighted the increased importance of the town.

Driven by a powerful and often blunt chief executive, Ernest Mexter, they pressed for every expansion opportunity and invested £millions in the infrastructure of the area including the Southern Orbital Road, which opened up acres of poor agricultural land for development.

Substantial expansion plans for the town had been a constant promise but the real start of the success story had waited until the 1950s.

Early in the century a scheme had been floated for the development of Ashford Garden City, a development starting with 300 new homes in Willesborough on a site which later became home to the North Schools and the former Town Football Club in Essella Road.

That failed to materialise, as did the 1947 government New Towns Act that studied the town for expansion but rejected it as a major project. It was the Town Development Act passed in 1952 to cater for the needs of expansion in towns that provided the kick-start and became the blueprint for the modern Ashford.

It was a decision that divided the community. Half wanted to keep the market town image with just one major industry – the railway works. The rest demanded modern workplaces, homes and career prospects. It was a major political issue, debated back and forth in the Elwick Road council chamber for years until the Labour party won control of the urban authority in 1957 and the go-ahead was given.

It was an historic moment in the history of the town in September 1959 when council chairman Cllr Charles Thomas signed the agreement to take London overspill.

Ashford pledged to build 5,000 houses over 15 years with only 750 reserved for locals. Provision was made for the creation of industrial estates with companies encouraged to move from the city to provide employment for the newcomers.

In 1957 Batchelors Foods (now Van den Burgh Foods) was the first major company to open in town with a £2 million food factory designed to process locally-grown vegetables. They proved to be a trailblazer of the new mix of industries, which quickly made the town such an attractive and popular place in which to work and live.

Slow and steady expansion has continued ever since, although there have been some major fears that the pace of progress could become too rapid. This was most evident in 1967 when Professor Colin Buchanan proposed developing a vast area to the south stretching as far as Hamstreet to house an additional 150,000 people, converting Ashford to a major city of a quarter million residents by the turn of the century.

The new city plan was rejected by the government, but at the time it was agreed that expansion on a more limited scale would continue. It did, and has, with

considerable success and hopes was particularly high when the area was nominated as Kent's Growth Town for the Eighties.

Business parks expanded and office developments indicated that the prosperous growth to bring a 'Boom Town Ashford' was well on target – until the closing of Chatham Dockyards diverted many companies to the opportunities being offered in the Medway Towns.

It was something of a blow but the announcement of the Channel Tunnel took the town full circle. The area was able to return to one of its major strengths, the importance of the railways, as a key to the future.

Ashford fought for the Eurotunnel consortium to win the construction project against all other developers because it was the only one to include an International Passenger Station in town. Again it was a long, hard fought battle won in the face of major opposition, but one which has put the town firmly on the European map.

Ashford Urban District councillors, meeting in 1929, were already discussing expansion as they prepared to take on the parishes of Kennington and Willesborough.

For many years Ashford council chamber stood as a town centre focal point in Middle Row in a building which also was home to the old fire brigade and public conveniences. The block was the original town Assembly Rooms underneath which were market stalls. These rooms were built in 1820, but the new front with balcony and council chamber were added in 1927. At the

time the chamber was also used for the monthly County Court. When this picture was taken in October 1958, the council was deciding to move to Elwick. Road and lease the building for conversion into shops and offices which remain to this day.

The historic signing of the London overspill agreement in 1959 was made by urban council chairman Cllr Charles Thomas. Watching him (from left to right) are Geoffrey Redfern (clerk to the council), the Rev W. Clarke (council chaplain), Arthur Ruderman (treasurer), and Mrs H. A. Coleman (vice-chairman of the council).

West Ashford councillors line up for a farewell picture with the staff shortly before the rural authority was amalgamated. Several councillors – Major Arthur Palmer, Harold Hilder, Major Bill Cotton and Mrs Win Swaffer – went on to be elected to the new authority and were among those responsible for much of its early success. Both majors served as mayors in the early years of the new borough.

The final meeting of East Ashford Rural District Council was held in the Elwick Road council chamber in March 1974 under the chairmanship of Peter Boulden who was later to become the first mayor of the new borough. His vice-chairman, Gordon Fortescue, and Cllr Jim Smith also served as mayor of the new council. From the ranks of officers, treasurer Fred Winslade became a long-serving borough and county councillor. Standing (from left to right): K. A. Pilkington (surveyor), J. H. Maurice (chief health inspector), K. Webber (clerk), Cllr P. G. Boulden, F. L. Winslade (treasurer), Cllr G. W. Fortescue, Cllr T. H. Jeanes. Sitting (from left front): Cllrs N. Funnell, Mrs C. Grace, Mrs N. Golding, W. E. Arter, G. Glover, R. W. Stocks, Mrs I. Oetzmann, Mrs J. Kiss, Mrs K. Dawes, M. Windsor, Mrs M. M. Tucker, J. F. E. Smith, N. H. Spearman, P. Baldwin, F. P. Lusted, C. Boulden, Mrs J. Linsert and Mrs A. F. B. Cottrell.

Well known and respected farmer Councillor Peter Boulden and his wife were the first mayor and mayoress of Ashford Borough Council when it was incorporated in April 1974.

Elected members and senior officers at the final meeting of Ashford Urban Council in 1974. Many went on to serve the new expanded authority with distinction and it is interesting to note that five of the councillors – Deryck Weatherall, Derek Madgett, Brian Prebble, Bernard Moorman and Gordon Turner – held the office of mayor in the early years of the new borough. Front row (left to right): Mrs Margaret Walker, Tony Russell, Mrs Mable Smith, Mrs Elsie Mayhew, Deryck Weatherall, Ernest Mexter, Mrs Peggy Ruffle, and Sydney Ford. Centre: Maurice Deeprose, Arthur Ruderman, Christopher Knight, Ray Colley, Bernard Moorman, Peter Holdstock, Michael Thompsett, Derek Madgett, William Williams, and Gordon Turner. Back: Harold Smith, Brian Prebble, John O'Connor, Dennis Mortimer, Stan Hammond, Geoffrey Redfern, Ray Knight, and Wilfred Gower.

Many of the buildings in Elwick Road, pictured here in June 1975, were formerly the offices of East and West Ashford Rural Councils. They were recorded as the best examples of Victorian architecture in Ashford and a preservation order was placed on them before they were taken over for use by the new borough authority.

In March 1983 Ashford's new £4 million Civic Centre opened for business in Tannery Lane to replace the numerous offices scattered along Elwick and Church Roads. After a settling-in period the new headquarters was officially opened by the Duchess of Kent on 8 December that year.

Batchelors Foods were the first major factory to open in Ashford to start the new industrial revolution. The vision to attract a wide range of light industry saved the town from major unemployment problems when the shock closure of the rail works was announced.

Bad Munstereifel Road is now a busy highway to the developing business parks of Sevington. In this 1983 picture it was still farmland about to be converted into the first section of the Southern Orbital road.

It was a great relief to the village of Great Chart when the bypass was officially opened by Sir John Grugeon in 1984 and halted the constant steam of A28 traffic through the narrow village street.

Health Matters

WHEN the long-fought campaign to site the new regional hospital in Ashford was won in the 1970s, residents were quick to celebrate the coming of the William Harvey facilities at Lacton.

It was indeed a major step forward in health service provision with most facilities at last concentrated on one site, including the long demanded accident and emergency unit.

Previously, accident victims had been forced to travel to Canterbury and many died en route along the A28 to the city.

Maternity services had been concentrated at Willesborough Hospital between Silver Hill Road and Kennington Road, which was transformed on closure to an industrial park of factory units. The buildings on this site were erected in 1835 and it was previously used by the East Ashford Poor Law Union.

Hothfield Hospital cared for the elderly; the Warren isolation hospital, built in 1860 as a private venture by local surgeon Henry Whitfeld was used for the treatment of cholera and smallpox and closed in the 1970s; and the main hospital and nursing quarters in King's Avenue which remained only to back-up facilities as the Harvey complex developed in phases.

Few may realise that the splendid new hospital opened in 1979 was the third to serve Ashford this century.

The original Ashford Hospital was in Wellesley Road on the corner of Hardinge Road and still stands privately owned and renamed Caxton House and used as offices.

Ashford Cottage Hospital built by the firm Giles and Burden of New Street, Ashford, for £2,645, opened in 1877. It was erected as a gift of local banker William Pomfret Burra in memory of his wife Isabella who died in August 1876, aged 46.

The first hospital secretary was Burgess Headley and locals were quick to respond to his appeals for money to equip the new building, which was built in

sections and eventually had an operating theatre and a children's ward.

Before this development, treatment of illness was at St John's House in Station Road, which was funded by subscription by a group of public-spirited individuals.

This opened in January 1870 with 14 beds available and the *Kentish Express* reported supporters included Sir Edward Hoare, Mr Charles Pemberton Carter and especially Mr John Furley.

The house was dependent on gifts for survival. They were recorded as taking the form of old linen and vegetable marrow. Records reveal that the maximum daily expenditure on vegetables was set at one shilling.

At first patients were taken to the makeshift hospital by cart. Then the purchase of an ambulance carriage for £20 made journeys for the sick slightly easier and it was reported that after much argument it was agreed to spend another £10 on a second carriage for infectious cases.

The press credited John Furley with the conception of the idea and a large share of the work in raising funds and planning the first home of treatment in Ashford.

John Furley, later Sir John, was born in 1836 in North Street the son of a local solicitor who started the still surviving firm of Halletts in Bank Street. He was involved in the formation of the St John Ambulance Association with its main aim being the teaching of first aid.

His life-long efforts for the sick started after witnessing the suffering the wounded faced during the Crimean War. He also designed stretchers and ambulances and during both the South African War and World War One he designed hospital trains to transport the sick and wounded to safety.

The Ashford St John Ambulance Corps, founded in 1879, is the oldest existing and now meets at headquarters at Barrow Hill, appropriately named Furley Hall when opened in 1960, from where they continue to give invaluable service in both training and providing voluntary cover for major events. He was knighted for his efforts in 1899 and died 20 years later.

Back at the Cottage Hospital by 1925 it became obvious that a new site was necessary such was the demand for services.

This hospital had only 38 beds and they were almost always fully occupied. The 1924 records show that 788 patients were admitted and that 523 operations had been carried out.

In those days no public funds were available so another appeal was launched in October 1925 and the response was so great that by June the following year tenders were invited for the erection of the new hospital in King's Avenue.

Hamstreet builders Messrs Godden & Sons were appointed to construct the hospital for £29,481, and on 20 October 1926, the Duke and Duchess of York (later King George VI and Queen Elizabeth) came to lay the foundation stone.

Many still remember that day when the Royal party were met at Ashford station by council officials and the Duke was taken to switch on the current for the town's new electricity supply. Then both the Duke and the Duchess toured the railway works site before lunch and in early afternoon laid the stone on the front elevation of the new building.

The people of Ashford responded to raise the funds and the most modern hospital design of the day, by Ashford architect Mr E. A. Jackson, was opened on 1 July 1928. Five years later the Old Cottage Hospital was auctioned and it was for some time the Ashford Inland Revenue office before being divided into a complex of office units a state it still retains today.

Fund raising continued to support the development of services and in November 1930 a Nurses' hostel was opened by Princes Helen Victoria and five years later a night nurses' hostel was completed. The whole operation was taken over by the National Health Service on 6 July 1948.

Ashford Cottage Hospital at the turn of the century.

King George VI, when Duke of York, laid the foundation stone of Ashford Hospital in King's Avenue, on 20 October 1926, when, together with Queen Elizabeth (later the Queen Mother, then Duchess of York), he also toured the railway works.

Ashford Corps St John Ambulance Cadets pictured in 1931.

Renamed Caxton House, the former Cottage Hospital continued to thrive as an office complex in this 1972 picture.

The William Harvey Hospital in September 1980, opened after a long battle for a regional hospital in town and named after the world famous physician who was born in Folkestone in 1578. On opening it was a proud boast that there should be ample free car-parking space for staff, out-patients and visitors, but the evidence from this picture seems to confirm what quickly was to become reality and parking charges had to be introduced in an attempt to curb demand. It is also interesting to note in the top of the photograph that major construction work was starting on the M20 motorway to Folkestone.

Thousands of local babies started their lives in the Victorian buildings of Willesborough Maternity Hospital, but in January 1982 the three-and-half acre site was sold to developers after Environment Minister Michael Heseltine over-ruled a public inquiry inspector and gave the go-ahead for its use as an industrial estate of 42,000 square feet of old and new factory units.

The Town Centre

TWO things changed the face of central Ashford – Hitler's blitz during World War Two and the coming of the notorious ring road in the 1970s. Numerous streets of solid homes along with long standing small businesses crumbled under demolition as planners pressed forward towards a dream of a vibrant traffic free central shopping and business area. The sound of the bulldozer and pneumatic drill was to become more familiar that bird song in the 1970s.

The council was constantly producing new traffic flow proposals and new sections of roads were being phased into operation in a major effort to combat the gridlock conditions that often existed.

The infamous ring road became a free-for-all speed circuit for the boy racers, and a potential death trap fear for those not familiar with high-speed lane changing manoeuvres. It brought stories of protest, which continued for years despite efforts to calm traffic by re-introducing traffic lights, which had disappeared five years previously, on some junctions.

Even those in authority would perhaps agree in hindsight that the route of the road was perhaps too near the central area in view of the expected expansion of the town, but it must be accepted that what was built did achieve the objective of preventing the traffic jams.

With the improvements came town centre expansion. The most concrete evidence of the new look central area came when mining giants Charter Consolidated relocated from London and opened Charter House in Park Street in 1974. Nine storeys tall and big enough to accommodate 1,200 employees it was, and still is, Ashford's biggest office block.

These were the days when so much of the heart of old Ashford was ripped away. Modern shopping centres were in demand and the Tufton Centre was planned as the ultimate answer with its variety of modern shops under expansive cover.

It came in the name of progress as other traditional companies like the long standing Lewis & Hyland department store in New Rents made way for the new building.

Those in power feared that the town was sliding towards economic disaster and the Chamber of Trade was pressing for urgent action. They demanded that the council raise the profile of the town to beat the state of stagnation that had persisted for some time.

The blame was placed firmly on the council insistence in planning the population intake too far away from the centre, particularly in the direction of South Ashford, and leaving vast areas of Godinton and Singleton undeveloped. The call was for confidence in the future and the ending of a stop-go policy to be replaced by planned growth of the town with viable amenities.

Commenting on Ashford Development Plans for 1970 Ashford council Labour leader Charles Thomas showed his great vision for the future when he told the *Kentish Express*: 'Surely the Chamber of Trade is right when it talks of stagnation and urgency. A start must be made on the Hempsted Street shopping centre to make Ashford the shopping centre it should be.

'The ring road and car parking must be proceeded with urgently to reduce congestion in the town centre. The position worsens daily and the only answer is a traffic-free centre.

'It is the duty of everyone of all political persuasion and interest to insist that Ashford's future size is realistically planned so that the ridiculous system of adding little bits whatever the current whim dictates, is no longer allowed to create town centre problems.

'Ashford can have a great future if it faces it with courage and foresight, but at the moment it is heading for disaster.'

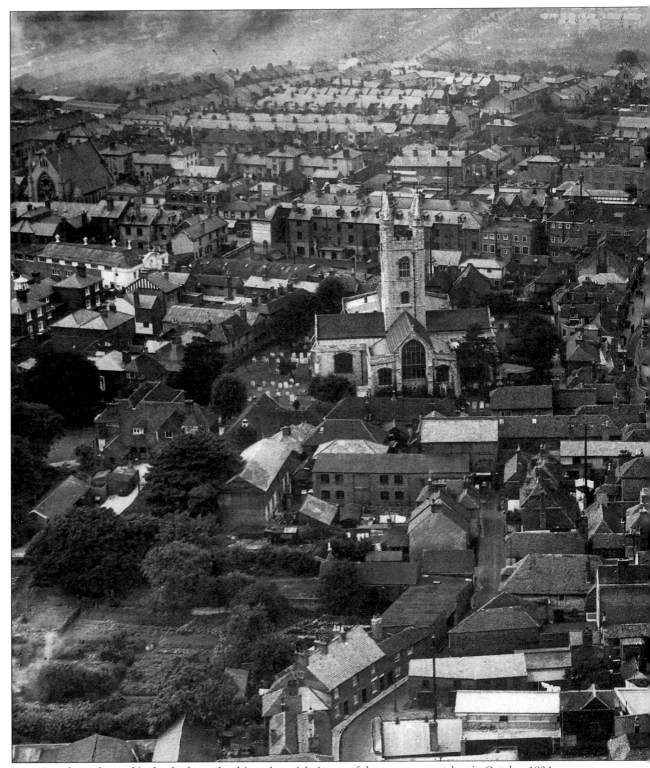

How times have changed is clearly shown by this early aerial picture of the town centre taken in October 1934.

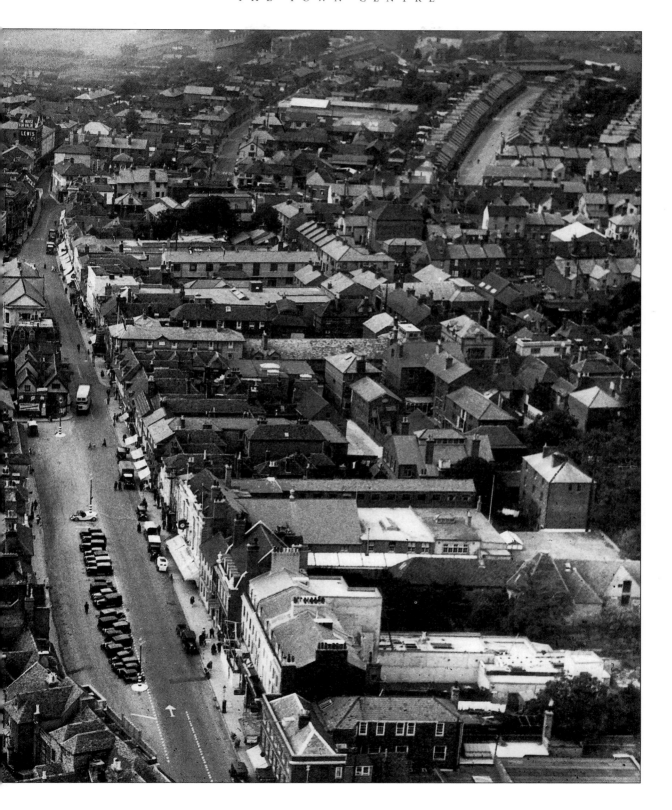

Lower High Street in the 1930s showing clearly number 46, the Headley grocer's shop. The family of Henry Headley took over this business in 1860 and it operated from the premises until 1976.

The upper High Street with trade bicycles much in evidence and F. W. Woolworth proudly claiming that they sold nothing over six old pence.

Pre-pedestrianisation Ashford was proud of the extreme width of the High Street, which this 1951 picture shows to perfection.

When the circus arrived in Ashford by train they paraded the animals through town. In this photograph the elephant line passes the Kent Arms at the bottom of Station Road which, as a Fremlins pub, was plastered with the brewery's elephant symbols.

For some years 69 High Street was home to the *Kent Messenger* newspaper but previously it had been an 18th century inn called, at various times, the Bull, the Naked Boy and the Star, and it is thought that at one time cockfights were staged at the pub. Bowketts the bakers, next door in this picture, was also a former inn known as the King's Head, and was also at one time used as the Post Office.

Historic Middle Row, Ashford buildings converted to modern shops in 1967.

In the 1960s and 1970s, Ashford had a top-class selection of quality town centre grocers including C. V. Crump and Headley Bros, but is Hudson's at 19 High Street that is fondly remembered as the last survivor until it closed in 1974 and was converted into Ashford's first Wimpy Bar. The shop was run by John Worger from the early 19th century and later by a family called Sankey, who held the Royal Warrant to supply the Duke of Edinburgh at Eastwell Park. In the final 30 years, when these pictures were taken, the business was run by Arthur Morris(left) and his son-in-law Cyril Raynes, who specialised in fine foods and boasted a selection of over 60 varieties of cheese in stock at all times.

Upper High Street looking towards Castle Street in 1970.

Her Majesty Queen Elizabeth II with the Duke of Edinburgh, Prince Andrew and Princess Anne, escorted by Canon Neville Sharp, were introduced to churchwarden Percy Woods and other church officials in 1970, after the celebrations to mark the 500th anniversary of the re-building of Ashford. Parish Church.

The final service before the demolition of the Ashford Congregational Church on the corner of Tufton Street and Church Road, was held on 4 August 1971. Among the congregation were the Rev D. Hellyar and Mary Hellyar, Rosemary and Mary Crouch, Audrey, Bert and Frank Palmer.

Demolition in the name of progress. The Congregational Church on the corner of Church Road and Tufton Street went to provide the site for the new law courts.

Premises next to the National Westminster Bank in the lower High Street have been used by a variety of businesses. In 1972 it was trading as a very successful Tesco Ware and Wear store.

Traffic was still scarce on the main route to south Ashford and Romney Marsh pictured here at Trumpet Bridge in Beaver Road beside the former open-air swimming pool in May 1972.

In February 1973, Park Street, Ashford, was still a busy business quarter which linked North Street with New Street, with long established traders like Tom Camier motor-cycles and Henley's car showrooms. Both were closed under council compulsory purchase to provide for the central distributor road system.

In April 1973, pensioners in Park Road, and Kent and Sussex Avenues were protesting at the announcement that this, their local Post Office, was to be demolished for road works. It proved to be another battle lost for locals in their fight against progress.

This fine old town house in Church Road was saved from decay early in the 1970s when it was converted into offices. Now the renovated building, standing next to the Elwick Club and opposite the Library, is home to accountants Phipps & Co.

Ashford's Elwick Club in Tufton Street, closed in 1973 to make way for the entrance to the town's first shopping centre.

The splendid new Elwick Club, which still stands opposite the Library in Church Road.

The scaffolding-covered Charter House nearing completion for Charter Consolidated in 1974. Since the mining company moved out of town, the offices have never been fully occupied

From the air, the vast office complex under construction in 1974.

Open for business in 1975 – Charter Consolidated Ltd's Park Street, Ashford, British headquarters of the worldwide mining business.

A bird's-eye view of the town centre showing the Tufton Centre under construction (above the parish church) and still no hint of the Park Mall Shopping development which today covers much of the land to the right of the High Street.

February 1974 and work was about to start to untangle a muddle of road junctions. Plans were announced to create a huge roundabout and traffic islands, and to block Western Avenue where it joined Maidstone and Chart Roads.

It caused quite a stir when the first zebra crossing to have zigzag approach markings to prevent parking was introduced in Bank Street, Ashford, in a bid to reduce accidents in the busy shopping area.

The banner claims, "You Can't Beat a Good Film," but this photograph was taken in 1974 before Top Rank decided to convert the biggest and best cinema in town into a bingo hall.

The upper High Street was home to the International Stores supermarket, a popular destination for shoppers when this 1977 photograph was taken. However, it was demolished to create the entrance to the Park Mall Shopping Centre.

Parking charges have always been a major issue and they attracted protests in 1982 when Vicarage Lane prices were increased and included a daily charge for town centre parking of £2, which was considered outrageous.

Middle Row, Ashford, in 1983 just before traffic was banned after major concern over potholes caused by heavy vehicles servicing shops in the narrow street.

July 1983 and the message from Ashford Council was blunt. The public were told to use or lose the Middle Row taxi rank which was being poorly supported by residents.

Buildings from the old Hayward's Garage were flattened in New Street to make way for the building of the Safeway Store which started trading with great success but has sadly now closed.

A photograph of busy North Street, taken from the roof of the new Sainsbury store, which was built on the site of the old Saracen's Head Hotel. It clearly shows not only the pre-ring road traffic problems but also the old established and familiar businesses, like Gibbs furniture shop and the Lord Roberts public house, which were shortly to disappear under the redevelopment plans.

October 1985 and there was major activity north of the High Street as work started to transfer the site into what is now the Park Mall Shopping Centre.

A quiet corner of St Mary's, Ashford, churchyard, pictured in 1987 after the renovation of the railings.

Winter wonderland – Ashford lower High Street in January 1985.

Ashford lower High Street in 1988, before traffic was banned and street markets were introduced.

Lost Locals

IT WAS last orders please in numerous town centre pubs in the early 1970s as one-by-one they were lost to redevelopment.

Many still lament the loss of so many familiar haunts where locals gathered for a quiet pint of fine ale and decent conversation before the coming of theme pubs.

In spite of massive protests and public inquiry seven ancient inns were bulldozed to make way for ring road and shopping centres.

Perhaps the most significant lost in the name of progress was the Lord Roberts which stood on its North Street site for 283 years. For two centuries it existed as the Red Lyon until it was renamed after the British General of the Boer War early this century.

In the same wave of demolition locals saw the closure of The British Flag in Forge Lane; The Park Hotel, in Wolseley Street; The Duke of Marlborough on East Hill; the Somerset Arms in North Street; and both the Wellington and the Coach and Horses in Hempsted Street.

Ashford Licensed Victuallers Association was outraged. They fought and lost a plea for preservation and demanded that replacement inns be developed.

The first major change had come seven years earlier when the Saracen's Head was demolished in 1967 to make a site for the new Sainsbury's supermarket on the corner of the High Street and North Street. That store then moved to the Park Mall shopping centre and the site is now home to Boots the Chemist.

As a leading hotel and meeting place, the original building was believed to have been constructed in 1478, but re-built in the mid 1800s, at which time it was used as a part-time base for local magistrates courts.

Sadly the decline has continued with the closure of the Invicta in Godinton Road; The Castle in Castle Street; and the Market, which was later renamed the Wig and Gavel, in Bank Street.

Perhaps, most surprisingly, the LVA plea was answered with the opening in the Tufton County Square shopping centre of the Zodiac pub which has since closed.

The Somerset Arms on the corner of North Street and Somerset Road was a victim of the ring road development.

The Saracen's Head Hotel, a former coaching inn on the comer of High Street and North Street, which was pulled down to make way for the town's first Sainsbury's superstore and later the site of Boots the Chemists.

The Park Hotel in Wolseley Road in 1971 before closure and demolition as part of the site of the Park Mall Shopping Centre.

It may not have looked like a typical pub but the British Flag in Forge Lane had a reputation for serving the best Fremlins bitter in town. The building dated from the mid-1840s when it was erected for the British School, which in 1856 had a roll of 292 pupils and was fast expanding. In 1862 the school moved to larger premises in West Street and the building was sold to the brewery.

June 1972 and one of the final pictures of the Wellington public house which stood on the corner of Hempsted Street.

The Duke of Marlborough pub in May 1972, still standing proudly at the top of East Hill, before demolition as part of the ring road scheme.

When news broke that Ashford's second oldest remaining pub was to be closed there were protests and petitions to save the Lord Roberts in North Street. But the developers won the day and it was demolished shortly after this 1974 picture was taken.

The Market Hotel in May 1975, which later changed its name to the Wig and Gavel, before being pulled down to make way for re-development. The building on the corner of Bank Street and Godinton Road opened in 1858 to serve the needs of those using both the nearby cattle market and corn exchange. The name change was presumably to tempt trade from solicitors and auctioneers from their Bank Street offices.

Popular hosts Edward and Lily Cager outside the Coach and Horses pub in Hempsted Street before it closed to make was for the construction of the Tufton Shopping Centre which was later re-named County Square.

Fire Services

ASHFORD had the first volunteer Fire Service in the country. Formed at a meeting of parishioners in the vestry room of Ashford Parish Church in January 1826, it was decided to launch an Ashford Fire Engine Association.

In 1836 a manual engine was purchased, in 1897 the first steamer and by 1925 they had the first Leyland motor fire engine. They provided a remarkable service to the town and there is some evidence that a volunteer service existed from 1814 with an 'engine' kept near the church which had nothing more than wooden rollers for traction and was hardly mobile in an emergency.

At first the Association service was stationed in Gravel Walk and all the money for engines and equipment was raised by public subscription. In 1876 it moved home to New Street, and in 1894 into the High Street at King's Parade. With two horse-drawn engines on call several horses were needed and they were stabled opposite at the Saracen's Head hotel.

It was early days but they installed a most modern electric call out system to the homes of fire crew and to both the Saracen's Head and the police station. The town always fully supported the service and public subscriptions were over £124 during the year.

In many towns the fire service was maintained by insurance companies and they would only deal with properties in which they had an interest, hence the firemarks which exist outside so many premises, and one can still be seen in its restored state on the wall of Middle Row.

The local men were considered among the best fire fighters in the county and were called to cover blazes over a wide area including the fire at the eastern end of Canterbury Cathedral in August 1872. Perhaps the biggest incident they attended came in December 1903 when Olantigh House at Wye was destroyed, but they also attended Headley's Invicta Press in Edinburgh Road, Ashford, which was gutted in 1906 with £20,000 of damage caused in just one hour.

The high level of efficiency they reached can be shown from the many competitions they entered. Records show that they were champions of the south-east at the turn of the century and were only narrowly beaten in the final of the national competition.

It is interesting to note that the service adopted completely new uniforms of felt helmet, canvas tunic, belt and spanner in 1867. Twenty years later the felt headgear passed out of service to be replaced by brass helmets for its 18-strong crew. This remained the standard dress until 1935.

By 1924 the crew had increased to 20 men who had motor, steam and manual appliances under their control with two fire escapes and a hose tender. To mark their centenary members formed a guard of honour for the Duke and Duchess of Kent when they visited the town to lay the foundation stone at the new hospital.

It was a sad day for many in 1943 when the volunteers ceased to exist when they were absorbed into the National Fire Service. In 1948, under the Fire Service Act, the Ashford Fire Brigade then became part of Kent Fire Service.

Eleven years later new fire headquarters, built at a cost of £25,000, were opened at Bybrook, Kennington, by Sir Edward Hardy, from where the needs of Ashford were covered until the recent move to an expanded site at Henwood.

The Steamer, pulled by prancing horses, speeds down North Street from Ashford Fire Station in King's Parade before the turn of the century.

Ashford's volunteer firemen were very much picture postcard heroes in the district and are seen here fighting a fire in about 1904.

Ashford Fire Brigade proudly mount their new Leyland Motor Engine appliance in 1925.

The major fire at Ashford Co-operative Store, which was practically burnt out in the lower High Street in 1926, was one of many incidents tackled by the volunteer firemen.

Firemen found time to pose for pictures inside the damaged Co-op store after the 1926 blaze.

After the Co-op blaze the gutted building in the lower High Street, pictured here, was brought back into use with remarkable speed.

The fire brigade sets off for another blaze on their motor fire engine in the early 1920s. At that time the fire station was in King's Parade and a call-out made a fine sight for shoppers as the firemen clanged their way through town centre traffic.

In 1959, Kent Fire Brigade opened a fine new £25,000 headquarters at Bybrook.

Gutted by fire in the 1970s, the 1901 flour mills at the foot of East Hill was converted into the town's first nightclub, complete with a pub, restaurant and function rooms.

A blazing East Hill Mill in 1974, which has been restored and converted into an entertainment complex.

Ashford's last remaining flour mill was wrecked by a £2.3 million blaze in 1984. The Victoria Road mill was owned by H. S. Pledge.

Trio of Treasures

IT WOULD be easy to dismiss Ashford as having little of great note which is worthy of preservation and certainly much has gone in the almost relentless pursuit towards the next century. What is left is almost entirely to the credit of a relatively small, but extremely determined number of residents, and in fairness to a number of elected councillors and officials, committed to the remaining of historic landmarks.

The grand old fountain in Victoria Park may soon play again thanks to lottery aid for its restoration after years of vandalism and decay. There is little doubt that this spectacular water feature could become a major attraction in an area of the town sorely neglected for so much of the century.

Plans to restore the park to its former grandeur to mark its centenary are in hand and the latest facelift comes not before time as it has been constantly underused. It was among the first area leased by the town board for sporting facilities in the days before the council.

From the Jemmett family in 1886 were rented 17 acres of parkland for sports and another area in Beaver Road for the swimming pool, which was to become one of the biggest and most popular outdoor pools in Southern England. Sitting as a member of that forward thinking board was antique dealer and furnisher George Harper, who was later one of the first elected members of the urban council when it was formed in 1894.

Four years later the council bought both the pool for an unknown sum, and Victoria Park which cost £2,870, with Cllr Harper always an enthusiastic supporter of the development of facilities which included the addition of a park bandstand in 1901.

It was the Hubert Fountain, which he presented to the town in 1910, that was always to be the pride and joy of the park where it still stands defiantly. A mid-19th century French fountain in painted cast iron its style is officially described as 'exuberant' in the list of buildings of special architectural and historic importance drawn up by the Environment Ministry.

It is listed as Grade II and described in the following terms: 'The topmost jet and bowl are supported by four cherubs standing on a plinth decorated by the masks of ancients. Below this are four bowls supported by two Gods and two Goddesses, which appear to represent four Continents, having attendant cupids with couches and cornucopia. Before this again, grotesque mask waterspouts eject the water into the basin'.

The fountain probably made its first appearance at the Great Exhibition in London's Hyde Park in 1851. After that exhibition some of the works of art were moved to a 22-acre site leased by the Royal Horticultural Society, near what is now the Royal Albert Hall in Kensington. It certainly appeared in an illustration of the gardens when Prince Albert opened them in 1861 according to newspaper reports.

Subsequently interest in the gardens declined and the fountain was sold for £3,000 to John Samuel Wanley Sawbridge Earl-Drax, otherwise known as the Mad Major of Wye, who installed it in his grounds at Olantigh Towers.

He gained his nickname as a result of his eccentricities. For instance, in the 1860s, he conducted a rehearsal for his own funeral and as MP for Wareham in Dorset he changed his name by royal assent by adding the Earl-Drax.

By 1912 he had tired of his exotic garden ornament and sold it to George Harper who gave it to the town, but even that caused conflict because the council refused to accept it because of the cost of moving it into position.

So after much haggling generous George paid to have his gift transported in manageable parts by horse and cart, traction engine and hand carts from Wye to south Ashford for erection, on condition that on his birthday each year – 23 July – the fountain was turned on to display its full glory.

It was on the day following his 71st birthday that it was formally presented to the town in 1912. Sadly Mr Harper was unable to attend through illness and the *South Eastern Gazette* reported that on behalf of her uncle Mrs Miles had turned the key controlling the water supply and delivered an excellent speech. Miss Knowles, granddaughter of the council chairman, had presented her with a bouquet, and the Buffs' had played a selection of music for the large gathering.

Sadly Mr Harper never lived to see if they kept his birthday wish as less than a month later on his usual morning stroll to The Warren, for unknown reason, he laid on the railway track and committed suicide under the wheels of the 11am from Cannon Street.

At the outbreak of World War Two in 1939 it ceased working and the graceful stags, which adorned it were removed, supposedly for their lead as wartime salvage. There were reports that they had been smuggled away and hidden in an area of Hillyfields but no trace of them has been heard of since.

The gradual decline continued with one of the last reports of it being used for the Coronation of Queen Elizabeth. It was most appropriate that to mark Her Majesty's Silver Jubilee a major project was launched to get it back in working order and at noon on 3 June 1977 Ashford Mayor Cllr Brian Prebble brought the fountain into play once again.

But again the joy was short as vandals damaged both the electrics and pump equipment, which left it unused for more decades.

Ashford's British Mark VI World War One tank was another gift to the town which was not always kindly received. It was presented in recognition of the citizens outstanding efforts in supporting the war loans campaign.

At its maximum speed of 3.7mph on 1 August 1919 it trundled noisily up the lower High Street preceded by a parade of scouts and cubs and led by a military band, to its resting place in St George's Square.

Known simply as Tank No 245, it was built around 1916 and is a female tank with five machine guns – two on each side and one at the front – and is now a listed building. It is one of only three still in existence.

Over the years it housed an electricity sub-station although now it is preserved in considerable style with a protective covering.

But when it first arrived this now much-loved feature of historic Ashford was not popular and readers were writing to the *Kentish Express* suggesting that the council transport it to Victoria Park and plant thickly growing shrubs closely round the unsightly object.

But the council resisted public pressure and the tank has become a prominent and popular feature.

The fully-restored working smock mill at Willesborough now stands proudly to the credit of all involved in saving this historic landmark.

Built in 1869 the Grade II listed building forms a significant part of the town's industrial heritage but its rescue from decay is a story of individual dedication to preserve the past supported by staunch council support.

In its heydays the octagonal wooden tower supported on a brick base was powerful enough to turn four millstones. Three years after it was built a steam engine was added which allowed it to continue working even when the wind dropped. In 1912 the steam boiler was replaced by an oil-fired engine, and in 1938 electric power was introduced.

It was a near perfect working mill until the sails, or sweeps, stopped turning in the 1950s and it was used for storage and as a home which over the next 30 years dilapidated under private ownership.

After years of High Court battles with organ-restorer owner Tom Robbins, who was required to return the building to working condition but failed due to the enormous costs, a compulsory purchase order was served for the council to take over responsibility and restoration, in the late 1980s.

After £40,000 repairs it is now run by the Friends of Willesborough Mill and visitors can step back into a by-gone age to discover how corn was ground and flour was made.

In the adjacent barn is a wheelwright's shop, museum pieces from Ashford's industrial past, and examples of the Norman Cycles made with such success in the 1950s.

Now, with a team of enthusiastic volunteers, the mill is set to expand as the centrepiece of a local heritage centre with a real hope that other threatened old buildings can be saved and re-erected on the ancient Mill Lane land.

It was the pride of Ashford and certainly for many years one of the town's most popular attractions. The outdoor pool in Beaver Road was one of the largest swimming centres in southern England and attracted major participation and crowds of supporters for the regular galas.

The Hubert Fountain in Victoria Park, pictured at the opening ceremony.

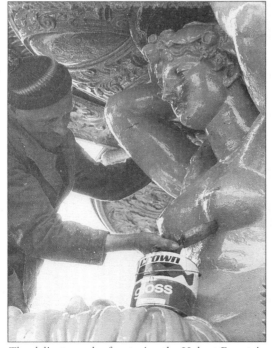

The delicate work of restoring the Hubert Fountain to its former glory in the early 1970s was quickly shattered by Victoria Park vandals who damaged both the electrics and pump equipment.

The Hubert Fountain in Victoria Park after restoration for Queen Elizabeth's Silver Jubilee.

A still working Willesborough windmill, with the village school in front in the days before it was left to decay and was almost lost to the town.

Fast decaying after years of neglect, Willesborough's old mill, pictured in 1980, was saved and restored by the council.

The restored Willesborough Windmill is now a familiar landmark for M20 travellers. Work by volunteers, supported by the council, has converted a building in danger of collapse into a major tourist attraction.

Crowds greeted the arrival of Ashford's British Mark VI World War One tank in 1919.

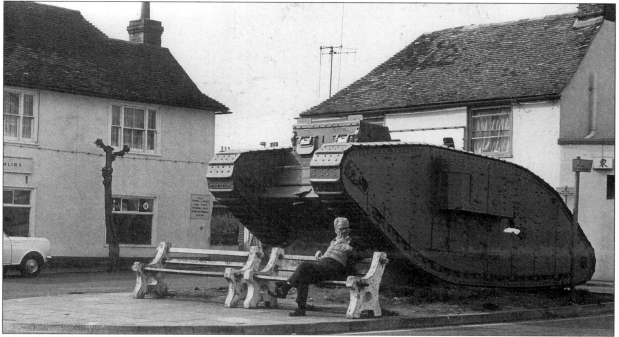

When the tank arrived in town, crowds packed St George's Square but over the years since it has often provided the backdrop for a place of quiet reflection.

The Housing Crisis

ASHFORD today has a wide choice of housing options to suit every need in terms of location, style and indeed cost. The whole area has a number of designated communities such as Kennington, Willesborough, Newtown, and South Ashford with a variety of town houses both old and new and flats plus pre-war homes and terraced properties.

Since the Kent Structure Plan clearly identified Ashford as a major growth point several large sites, starting with Singleton and then Park Farm on the edge of Kingsnorth and later a series of other prime sites, have been earmarked for the future.

The council itself has in recent years led the way in encouraging housing association partnerships and been at the head of local needs housing provision in rural areas, but it was a different story back in the 1970s when the local authority faced a major scandal over their home building programme.

After a serious fire in Orion Way, Willesborough, in 1976 the council commissioned an independent architect to report on the state of timber-framed houses built between 1968 and 1975. Another expert was called to report on the electrical wiring and fittings in the same homes. Together the reports listed grave faults that would cost at least £2 million to correct.

Several council officials and many elected members were criticised in the debates that raged.

These homes in Beaver Lane, south Ashford, built in the 1920s, were among many demolished after structural faults were discovered.

October 1981 and a peaceful scene of new homes with carefully tended gardens in Orion Way, Willesborough.

Some of the blame was attributed to the fact that the town urgently needed new homes, as they were facing a critical shortage in 1967 as the impending ring road project involved the demolition of 149 properties, and an obligation to re-house those displaced.

A combination of shortage of bricks, and the speed of construction and cheaper cost of timber-framed building, led to the decision to rapidly build on a selection of sites in and around the town. What started as an investigation into an estate of 92 homes in Willesborough finished with almost 1,000 homes on the suspect list with many facing demolition or a complete re-build.

Throughout the borough tenants were on tenterhooks living in homes with design faults that had been declared as possible fire risks. The houses in Orion Way were the first named for demolition but a sizeable community stayed on the jinxed estate because of a lack of alternative accommodation.

Once these had been happy homes, until you remember that they had been designed and built, occupied and then doomed to destruction, all in the space of about five years.

There was much frustration and anger before all the doomed unsafe homes were replaced at enormous cost to the town, but the blow was later followed by the need to demolish another 120 homes built in the 1920s in Langholm Road and Beaver Lane after the discovery of structural faults.

It was all a far cry from the praise that was heaped on the authority for the £2 million modernisation of Newtown in 1975.

Following a long, and at times bitter, fight by the Newtown Action Group under the formidable leadership of Theresa Crow, flats and homes more than 100 years old were either replaced or upgraded. Hot water and all modern amenities were installed leaving tenants singing the praises of the council for their imaginative planning and supervision of the project.

Ashford's growing prosperity was attracting a new breed of both developers and 'yuppie' homebuyers in the late 1980s. But on the other side of the coin the situation facing hundreds of forlorn working families was getting serious. There was another housing crisis with almost 100 families designated as homeless and almost 2,000 on the council house waiting list.

To add to the problems residents in south Ashford found that their homes were built on an old rubbish tip and the decomposing waste was releasing highly flammable methane gas.

Residents of Halstow Way were shocked but resigned to moving out and once more the bulldozers moved in to remove yet more modern homes from the town housing stock.

Some of the doomed homes in Orion Way, Willesborough, in 1981, pictured before demolition.

Weeks later all 114 homes on the estate had to be demolished after serious design faults were discovered and the council decided it would be safer and cheaper to rebuild rather than repair.

Twinning Links

IT IS quite remarkable that the town that suffered such horrific death and destruction from the Germans during World War Two, should form successful friendships which have survived and expanded every generation since.

Ashford's twinning links with the Rhineland town of Bad Munstereifel were among the first established between the United Kingdom and Germany after the conflict, and they have been recognised as an example of all that is best in international friendship.

The roots of this amazing determination to forgive, but never forget, and rebuild for peace and solidarity, lie with former Mayor of New Romney, Alderman John Wiles who lived in Ashford and is buried in the town cemetery.

In service in the Eifel region after the end of the war he first experienced the warmth of the friendship from the citizens of the ancient walled town with which Ashford was to form the official link. He made many friends, including teacher and ex-Luftwaffe officer Ferdinand Lethert, who had been shot down and captured in North Africa and spend most of the war as a prisoner in America.

Together they discussed the stupidity of war and the need for future generations to extend friendship beyond national boundaries. As a result it was just seven short years after the war that Ferdi Lethert brought the first German-English Youth Exchange party to Kent, and his family has been organising the trips for students every year since.

To mark his distinguished and devoted service to Anglo-German relationships he received the MBE from the Queen in 1964 – when he was one of the first Germans to receive an honour. A decade later his own country decorated him with the Federal Order for Distinguished Service.

In 1986 to mark his massive efforts towards the friendship he was made the first individual Freeman of the borough of Ashford, the highest honour the town can bestow on an individual.

It was a reflection of the universal affection for Ferdi Lethert, a man of the people equally at home at major civic occasions, or with the working man in the bars of local pubs, that it was a unanimous decision to honour a foreign citizen for his services to Ashford.

The town is rightly proud of its official European links. Formal twinning with the mediaeval spa centre, which is listed as an historic monument, took place in the summer of 1964 with much pomp and ceremony in Germany.

The following year in Ashford one of the block of flats in Bybrook, Kennington, was named after Herr Huel the giant Burgermeister who led the official delegation to complete the twin link. It is interesting to note that among the places of pride visited by the officials was a tour of the new sewage works!

In the years that followed Ferdi Lethert House for elderly people was developed in Kennington and later Burgermeister Heinz Gerlach named another complex and the new southern orbital road was named Bad Munstereifel Way.

Three years later the Germans twinned with Fougeres in Brittany but the completion of the triangle of friendship provided considerable conflict and debate. It took a rocky six-year engagement called a 'liaison amicale' before the formal marriage with the French and the long-awaited completion of the signing of the official scrolls in 1984.

Perhaps the biggest honour came in 1987 when Ashford was awarded the European Flag of Honour for outstanding effort to promote European unity. Then it was stressed that the future of twinning lay in the hands of Ashford youth to be part of the heart, soul and spirit of Europe, and that the flag was a symbol of the long journey towards tolerance and understanding of other people and their cultures.

Like all partnership towns and cities Ashford has its entrance signs announcing the links. It also has a most visible reminder of the agreement with a six-and-a-half ton lump of basalt quarried in the

Rhineland and transported 300 miles to stand in the pedestrianised lower High Street as a symbol of friendship between the three towns.

The erection was supervised by Herr Lethert and it was unveiled by Bad Munstereifel Burgermeister Heinz Gerlach, during the highly-successful Twinning Week celebrations organised by Ashford Twinning Association in 1983.

This festival of friendship was just one of the numerous events staged by supporters of the twin town agreement that extends to all manner of sporting and cultural and social exchanges and visits between the trio of towns of bands, majorettes and individuals in additional to annual civic ceremonial.

Currently Ashford is preparing to formalise the growing links with Hopewell in Virginia. In 1623 Captain Francis Epps sailed on the good ship *Hopewell* for the new colony in America and was later given a royal land grant of 1,700 acres on the James River by King Charles I.

Francis Epps, the son of a wealthy Ashford landowner, was baptised in St Mary's parish church in 1597. In Virginia he served as a member of the House of Burgesses, as a the Commissioner for parts of the colony, and as a member of the Council of Virginia.

He founded one of the oldest plantations with its 18th century Appomattox Manor that had remained in the family until 1979 when it was acquired as a National Historic Site of America.

August 1964 and the start of the official friendship link when council chairman Charles Doe led the civic party to Bad Munstereifel to be greeted by Ashford and district teenagers on the annual English-German Youth Exchange, before the week long celebration ceremonies.

Mayor and mayoress Major and Mrs Arthur Palmer made the presentations to visiting leaders Helmut Cloot and Gunter Kirchner at Ashford Twinning Association dinner in honour of their German guests in 1975.

The twin town band from Bad Munstereifel on parade through the streets of Ashford during the September 1976 Carnival.

French and German twin town visitors were entertained at the restored Willesborough Windmill on one of the many civic visits by European friends to Ashford.

Burgermeister Heinz Gerlach hands over the twinning symbol to the town watched by Mayor Cllr Jo Winnifrith and Twinning Week chairman Bill Thomas.

Herr Ferdinand Lethert oversees the laying of the lower High Street Friendship stone.

The lower High Street during the 1983 Twinning Week celebrations which attracted major crowds anxious to extend the friendship links with the partnership towns of Bad Munstereifel in Germany and Fougeres in France.

Famous Names

MANY never consider the real significance of road names, as the majority are common to many towns. Almost all are blessed with Station, Church and London Roads, High, Queen's and New Streets, and others linking them to named adjacent settlements.

More than most Ashford has an interesting selection of both thoroughfares and buildings named after notable local residents.

One of the most recent is Simone Weil Avenue named in 1983 after the French authoress and philosopher who died in the nearby Grosvenor Sanatorium in 1943 and is buried in Bybrook cemetery.

Born in Paris in 1909 she has sympathy with the poor and worked as a manual labourer to experience working-class life. She served with the Republican Forces in the Spanish Civil War and in 1942 joined the Free French Government in London, but developed tuberculosis.

Brought to the Sanatorium her improvement was not aided by her insistence to eat only the same rations allowed to those in her occupied homeland and she soon died.

Since her death her thoughts have been published and they have established her as one of the foremost modern philosophers, and the French have presented her vintager's (grape gatherer's) hat to Ashford council. It is on permanent display at the Civic Centre.

At first glance it is difficult to see the link between Jemmett, William, Francis, Bond and Elwick Roads, but they can all be traced to the family of one of the towns most successful businessmen – George Elwick Jemmett.

In 1805 he bought the Manor of Ashford. George and his brother William came to the town in 1770. They were the sons of Caleb Jemmett of Maidstone and his second wife Ann who was the daughter of Robert Elwick, the Vicar of Bredgar.

The Jemmett family used Elwick as the second name for the next five generations to preserve the link. Not only were they lords of the manor but bankers of note and for much of the 19th century they were considerably involved in the development of the town.

They owned lands stretching throughout south Ashford south of the rail tracks and in that area were the four streets all named after members of the family. He also developed much of Bank Street, the lower part of which was known as George Street until 1880, and Elwick Road, with the areas taking his christian names.

The ownership of Ashford Manor passed down the generations with George Elwick Jemmett II and William Francis Bond Jemmett holding the title. In 1923 George Elwick Jemmett III died leaving three daughters (his only son George Elwick Jemmett VI was killed in the war).

Last member of the family recorded in Ashford was W. Jemmett the final manager of Jemmett's bank and the first manager of the Lloyds branch with which the old bank merged in 1902. It was located on the site where it still stands on the corner of the High Street at the entrance to Bank Street on the exact spot where the first George Jemmett owned a home when he bought the Manor of Ashford more than 100 years earlier.

In the days when everyone living in Newtown was totally involved in the railways, the significance of road names was clear and highly respected, but to newcomers the greats of the age of steam mean little – Stirling Road, Wainwright, Maunsell, and Bullied Places, all off Alfred Road, the original name for the New Town.

James Stirling was chief engineer at the works and chairman of the Association of Locomotive Engineers. In 1889 he took the gold medal at the Paris exhibition for one of his Ashford-built express locomotives.

He was followed by Harry S. Wainwright at the turn of the century who brought many of the improvements to conditions in the workshops and was credited with designing some of the top luxury carriages during what was a period of massive productivity at the base.

His successor in 1913 was R. E. L. Maunsell who as chief mechanical engineer designed the famous *Lord Nelson*, which at the time was considered the most powerful engine in the United Kingdom. On retirement he handed over to O. V. Bulleid whose major task was the supply of 'Austerity' armed locomotives for the War Department.

Each played an important part in the life of the town remembered in those simple nameplates.

The often wrongly-spelt Whitfeld Road in south Ashford is no doubt named after either surgeon of this town Henry Whitfeld, who in 1860 had the Warren isolation hospital built as a private venture, or Lewis Whitfeld a partner in the Ashford Bank with the Jemmett Brothers.

Both were greatly respected and the death of Henry in 1869, described as a local philanthropist, was widely reported in the press. Funds were raised by public description to build a hall in his memory which was opened in 1874 and still stands in Bank Street.

Magazine Road has a military connection but has nothing to do with gun ammunition. It was on the 1797 site where mounted units were stationed and the area was a store for oats for the horses and biscuits for the men. Beaver Road and Lane are not named after the animal but from the French 'beau voir' or beautiful view, although not much of it exists today.

Wallis Road is named after Dr John Wallis son of a Vicar of Ashford in 1916 who became a mathematician of considerable influence and was admired by such distinguished gentlemen as Sir Isaac Newton and diarist Samuel Pepys.

Boys Hall Road at Willesborough was named after Thomas Boys of Sevington who built Boys Hall as a family home in 1616. No doubt in days of old all were worthy of their public reward, but equally important are the more modern heroes, which attract more than a little notice.

How pleasant it much be for the sporting fanatic to live in the Highfield area of Willesborough on the development of Luckhurst Road with Woolmer and Shepherd Drives, Julien Place, Knott Crescent, Ealham, Jarvis, Cowdrey, and Johnson Closes, all named after those Kent cricketing stars of the 1970s. And for those who note that perhaps the greatest of them all is not included – Underwood Close already existed at Kennington.

The Knatchbull Family

AS head of one of Kent's oldest families Lord Brabourne is an inspirational film producer with many famous titles including *A Passage to India* and *Death on the Nile* to his credit.

His wife, the Countess Mountbatten of Burma, is an active patron or president of a staggering list of charities, plus a staunch supporter of many military, educational and community organisations.

Together they have played an important part in the life and times of the Ashford district for more than half a century, and one which with their close royal links has often turned the national spotlight on local events.

Countess Mountbatten is first cousin to Prince Philip and third cousin to the Queen. She is god-mother to Prince Charles, who in turn stood as godfather to her twin sons. The Queen is godmother to second son Michael-John Knatchbull, and Prince Philip is godfather to eldest son and heir Norton Knatchbull who is now Lord Romsey. The King and Queen of Sweden were among the other godparents of her seven children.

It was in October 1946 that Captain John Knatchbull and Lady Patricia Mountbatten married in Romsey Abbey in what was the society wedding of the year. He was wearing the uniform of the Cold-stream Guards and three Princesses – Elizabeth, Margaret and Alexandra of Kent - and her sister Pamela, were attending his future wife. Among those attending the ceremony were King George VI and Queen Elizabeth.

Both she and Lord Brabourne are clearly part of the royal social circle, although not technically members of the Royal Family, but they are also both deeply committed to the local community.

When first married they lived in Park Cottage, a small house in Smeeth, before moving to the somewhat misleadingly named Newhouse in Mersham village. It was in fact built as a Dower House

to be near the Tudor mansion in the park and it is here that so many royal guests have been entertained.

Lord Brabourne is part of the Knatchbull family, which settled in the area when Richard Knatchbull purchased Mersham-le-Hatch, a large Adam house in splendid parkland on the outskirts of town in 1486, as the ancestral home.

That the present family have never lived there is a tribute to the generations of family dedication to education and it still continues as home to the Caldicott Community, a foundation for the care and teaching of severely damaged and maladjusted children.

The estate now stretching to over 2,000 acres and one of the most successful in the area, is still managed by the family and attracting royal visitors for the top-class game shooting. As a family there has always been a special relationship with both tenant farmers and employees of the estate who were also included in the top social occasions.

It was in 1630 that Sir Norton Knatchbull founded Ashford Grammar School in the Ashford town centre churchyard building later known as the Dr Wilks Memorial Hall and now home to the Borough of Ashford Museum. He appointed a teacher at a salary of £30 a year. Norton was the first member of the family to be knighted and he represented Kent in Parliament from 1609, and he began a family association with education that still thrives.

Lord Brabourne has a remarkable record of outstanding service. He is Kent's longest-serving school governor, now in his 53rd year with more than 40 as chairman, of Norton Knatchbull School board.

His father-in-law Earl Mountbatten opened Ash-ford Boys Grammar school main school building in Hythe Road in 1968, and five years later the school was renamed Norton Knatchbull in honour of its founding family and Lord Brabourne buried a time capsule and laid the foundation stone for a major extension.

Prince Charles opened a new cricket pavilion in

Crowds lined the church approach on 5 April 1957 as Her Majesty The Queen and Prince Phillip joined Lord and Lady Brabourne for a service conducted by Rector, the Rev H. McDonald at Mersham Parish Church.

1980 and in 1992 Lord Romsey declared open the new school extension for maths, languages and sixth form facilities.

Lord Brabourne is also deeply involved with Wye College, and was one of the original sponsors and is still active with the University of Kent at Canterbury. Another

Her Majesty The Queen with Vicar of Smeeth, the Rev O. W. T. Evans leaves morning service at the Parish Church on 19 December 1958, followed by Princess Anne, the Duke of Edinburgh and Lord and Lady Mountbatten.

The Queen and Lady Braboume relax in deck chairs watching cricket at Mersham-le-Hatch.

great love is nature conservation, which is shared by the Countess whose voluntary responsibilities to the county are too numerous to mention.

Together their long-standing involvement in helping others less fortunate through charities and general good deeds in the district is almost legendary. To many they are regarded as life-long friends and when the long established and successful family life was shattered on August Bank Holiday in 1979 Ashford was left in shock and mourning.

The Countess's father, Earl Mountbatten of Burma, was assassinated by the IRA during a family outing on board a fishing boat off the Irish coast. The same bomb killed 14-year-old twin Nicholas Knatchbull, and Doreen, Lady Brabourne, Lord Brabourne's mother. It also severely injured Countess Mountbatten, Lord Brabourne and their other twin Timothy. It was a day Ashford will never forget.

In the weeks, months and years following the outrage, the Countess, Lord Brabourne and their son have all made excellent recoveries but the fight to mend the mental wounds inflicted by the cowardice of the action will never depart.

Typically, rather that back out of the public eye, as they would have had every right to do, they threw themselves into work with an enthusiasm that defies both their age and the ordeal they survived. There was a real hint of disappointment when the Countess was forced to stand down as a magistrate on reaching 70 after serving on the Ashford bench for 23 years, in 1994.

The Duke of Edinburgh proved to be a tricky spin bowler in a match at Mersham, and you can see the concern on the face of batsman Frank Wanstall as he prepares for a single and to then face the Prince.

A young Prince Charles with Lord and Lady Brabourne after he stood as godfather to the Knatchbull twins.

Youth Matters

YOUNG people in the district have always been more fortunate than those in most areas to have adult leaders willing to devote time and energy to supporting the interests of youth.

Whether it be with coaching of a wide variety of sporting excellence, heading the far ranging uniformed groups of scouts, cubs, guides, ambulance and red cross cadets, boys brigade or woodcraft folk, or running youth and theatre groups, Ashford has provided outstanding leadership.

One man – William James Morgan – perhaps above all, stands out as an example in a class of his own despite shunning personal publicity.

By nature a quiet, modest man he devoted his life to St Mary's Boys' Club and Youth Fellowship and constantly laboured for the good of Ashford youth as a whole. The rebuffs, setbacks and disappointments were many but his leadership style was always inspiring from the moment he rallied support to build the Bentley Road clubhouse in 1957.

He made great efforts to teach young people the values of international friendship and in those days of extreme political differences in Europe visitors from Russia and Germany were familiar and welcomed figures at his club events.

Somehow he seemed able to cope with frustration from bureaucrats and indifference and apathy from those in power to keep his club going and build on its growing reputation, but nothing could prepare him for the events of 21 August 1968.

He was leading a party of four adults and 20 boys and girls from the club on a goodwill stay in the Czechoslovakian capital of Prague. For the 24 Ashford people it was the day they were trapped in a communist invasion. For Bill Morgan it was his finest hour as he calmly planned and led the party to safety after three days of fear.

It was the club's third cultural and educational exchange with the Czechs and they had spent two happy days in the city visiting the sites and mixing with the locals who like them were quite unaware of the invasion plans.

Bill was one of the first to grasp the awful truth that the sleeping city was being invaded by Russians, East Germans, Polish and Hungarian troops when he was disturbed at 2am in his hotel near Wenceslas Square, and in the semi-darkness watched tanks, troop carriers and armed soldiers in the streets.

He confessed at the time that he was alarmed by the situation, but in the hours and days ahead he never let that fear develop into panic as he set about sustaining the confidence of his party and taking steps amid all the confusion to inform relatives that the party was safe.

Against a background of whining bullets, the thud of shells, the sickening slaughter, and all the horrifying nerve-destroying bedlam of invasion, he kept his cool, planning to make sure his group were on board the first train to safety out of the city.

He achieved his objective and then tried hard to shun the limelight for himself when they returned home to Ashford. The youngsters knew and respected their leader even more and the television pictures had shown the parents the intense reality of the dangers their youngsters had faced.

Modest Bill had served both the youth movement and the town with pride. His outstanding efforts over so many years should be remembered and it is particularly sad that the headquarters he worked so hard to achieve in his prime should become a victim of vandalism and lack of support that it was forced to close and has now gone for ever.

Off to camp in 1912. The 1st Ashford Scouts prepare to leave from outside Hanson's fish shop in New Street.

Mersham Panto was a regular treat for locals and this line-up is the cast of 1948 preparing for the latest performance on the village hall stage.

The building of St Mary's Youth Club in Bentley Road, Willesborough, brought a great deal of community participation. Above, urban council chairman Cllr Charles Thomas helps to unload the bricks for volunteers who were building the impressive and much needed clubhouse.

South Ashford Methodist Sunday School scripture exam winners posed for pictures in 1957. They were Keith Ades, Mrs Greenstreet, Mrs Kennett, Peter Oliver, Gordon Crust, V. Ammon, Neil O'Rourke, Miss E. King, Roy Osbourne, Mary Wright, Derek Osbourne, Pamela Wright, Eileen Osbourne, Barbara Cox, Mrs L. Ammon, Alan Wright, Michael Ammon, Colin Hockley, Susan Ammon, Carol Kennett, Maureen Cox, Margaret Kennett, John Adams, Michael Cox, Better Adams and Brian Powell.

The town centre Hollington Prep School is fondly remembered by many including this group of pupils in 1974.

Children's Day, which often went on well into the evening, was a major pre-Christmas tradition in Ashford High Street when families turned out in their thousands to greet the arrival of Father Christmas with festive carol singing, the switching on of the illuminations, entertainment by national stars... and the raising of money to help the old and needy. Here organiser Joe Fagg leads the musical entertainment in the 1964 procession and staff from Crouch's Garage pose with their 1962 float entry.

There is always a big turn out for the annual St George's Day parade through the town centre. This picture of the uniformed youth groups marching through the High Street is from 1974.

World Cup winning captain Bobby Moore was the star of Children's Day 1976 and crowds blocked the entire High Street for carol singing and entertainment led by girls pipers. Other stars to attract maximum crowds to this free fun event include singer and artist Rolf Harris and comedian Michael Bentine.

In November 1982 conditions at the North School for Boys (Lower School) in Hythe Road were described as disgraceful by local education watchdogs. They called for the sub-standard former Grammar School to be abandoned and new facilities provided. Teacher Les Lawrie reported that the building had been condemned as unsuitable for teaching accommodation for many years and after some years it was demolished.

In Conclusion

TAKE a bird's-eye view of the area and to the south of Willesborough and Sevington and you will see the biggest changes in the structure of the town taking place in a daily drive towards the turn of the century.

Ever since the opening of the £6 million southern orbital road linking Willesborough with south Ashford was completed, this south-east sector has been the critical area for development and the vision of planners, despite major protests in the early 1980s, is clear for all to experience.

That the council has a clear plan for the future has served Ashford well in the scramble for expansion. Quality companies are consistently being attracted to look to re-locate to the area served not only by excellent transportation links and local infrastructure, but by officials ready and willing to welcome new business partnership.

Flexibility, and a certain boldness in investing in the future during times of depression, has been the key to Ashford being on the threshold of success in the new century. It has, and will not come, without great imagination and at times conflict with local residents.

More than 1,000 from Sevington and South Willesborough signed petitions against the south-east sector development and hundreds turned out at protest meetings, but they lost the battle and now hundreds of acres of poor quality agricultural land has been released and is available, indeed much already being developed, for business and residential use.

It is the latest part of the town strategy started in the 1950s to encourage wide ranging job opportunities in the area ideally situated for modern industrial needs. The determination to build a strong and sustainable economic base is also reflected in the creation of the 80-acre Eureka Science Park beside the motorway and Warren with low-density high-tech development.

Together these may be the prestige large scale and most visible development sites, but that Ashford seriously means business and is determined to be a town with a future in the exciting years ahead, can be established by the wide selection of business parks and industrial estates to suit every size of business.

Everything has been done to encourage newcomers ranging from starter units to massive office blocks all available at competitive rents.

The strategy seems to be working with an influx of small French companies taking advantage of the Eurostar and Shuttle connections, and American firms led by the construction toy giant K'Nex choosing Ashford as their European base for packing and distribution of kit toys.

With a vast section of the old rail works at Kimberly about to be reborn into a 100-plus factory shopping centre, planned to attract two million visitors a year, we could have the catalyst for development in the surrounding area which could indeed bring back to life the whole of the former railway works.

And, if that takes off, Ashford has a blueprint for the future development of the town centre. Dover Place to Tannery Lane could become a European market square area with specialist shops, a budget hotel and youth hostel, family leisure facilities and craft workshops, and eventually a concert hall.

The South Kent College site on the corner of Station and Elwick Roads is earmarked as a site for European arts and culture with the possibility of a business school; the Vicarage Lane car park could be developed with retail stores and with leisure facilities; and Victoria Road could see hotel and conference facilities with office and business development.

They may be planners' pipe dreams but so too were many of the road schemes and development sites we all accept as normal now.

The important thing is that Ashford is ready, and willing, to enter the 21st century prepared to take every advantage of its excellent location at the hub of the road and rail network to both the UK and Europe.